THE JOY OF
BOCCE

5th Edition

By
MARIO PAGNONI

STRIKER

The Joy of Bocce, Fifth Edition

Copyright © 2010, 2011, 2015, 2017 by Mario Pagnoni

ISBN: 978-0-578-19060-0

Library of Congress Control Number 2017903511

The Joy of Bocce 5th Edition books are available at special discounts
when purchased in bulk quantities for businesses, associations, institutions,
special promotions or sales promotions. Please call our Sales Department at
978-686-8679 or order at JoyofBocce.com

Or contact our distributor:
Cardinal Publishers Group at 800-296-0481 or www.cardinalpub.com

STRIKER PUBLICATIONS
Email: Strikerpag@aol.com
Website: www.JoyofBocce.com

THE JOY OF
B🌑CCE

TABLE OF CONTENTS

To My Sons James and Joseph:
"You Made Me The Father I Am Today"

Acknowledgments

First and foremost, I must thank my father-in-law, Gennaro Daniele, who gave me my first set of bocce balls. This gift led to a love affair with the sport. After decades of baseball, basketball, jogging and many knee operations, bocce has become more appealing to me than ever. Many people submitted ideas and comments in additions to great photos. I can't begin to thank them all, but will mention a few who went above and beyond to make the final product what it is today.

I gratefully acknowledge the contributions of Clare Coco, Michael Grasser, Tom McNutt, Dave Brewer, Bede Kortegast, Richard Heisler, Linda Lemerise, John Ross, Jeff and Jack O'Heir, Michael & Lois Conti, Joe Giolli, Ron Jacobs, Michael Lapcevich, Elizabeth Jade Fontana, Dan Passaglia, Dr. Angel Cordano, Rico Daniele, Phil Ferrari, Donna Allen, Ken Dothee, Lou Ures, and Ralph Bagarella. All are bocce lovers of the highest order. In addition, special thanks go to Dianna DiStefano and James Pagnoni who contributed their immense talent for analyzing and selecting just the right photos to complement the text.

Finally, my heartfelt thanks go out to Brian Marquez who deftly designed the book's cover.

PREFACE

Bocce, though already catching on rapidly in this country, would really take off if it got the proper exposure. Hopefully this book will help. I'm not talking about it flourishing as a tournament event with complicated rules, state-of-the-art equipment, and high-powered authorities running (or ruining) the sport. I'm referring to a simplified recreational version that can be played by anyone almost anywhere. This game doesn't require great strength, stamina, quickness or agility. You don't need cat-like reflexes or the hand-eye coordination of an NBA backcourt man. Men and women as well as boys and girls of all ages can participate and enjoy the sport, making it as competitive or as laid back as they desire. It is well suited as a game for the countless physically challenged individuals worldwide because anyone who can roll a ball can play. Best of all, you don't need expensive equipment. And, played as described here, you don't even need a court - your back yard or neighborhood park will do nicely. You can play recreational bocce on grass or dirt, on level or uneven terrain - even at the beach (on the shore or on sandbars during low tide).

Bocce suffers from an image problem in America. People see it as an "old fogies' game" played at social clubs. The word bocce conjures up images of cranky old coots competing on customized outdoor courts. Arguing and kibitzing (sometimes even cursing - usually in Italian) and generally having a great time, these old-timers seem engaged in some sort of geriatric lawn bowling. It looks about as exciting as watching cactus grow in the desert. But it is a wonderful game, full of skill and strategy - one that requires finesse as well as some occasional brute force. This book attempts to dispel the misconceptions about bocce, and aims to promote it as a backyard game that is an ideal recreational activity for family cookouts, picnics, and other get-togethers. In addition, this book will help guide those who may want to take the game to the next level, whether it be the social club level, tournament action, or international play. Most of all, our goal is to get the word out on what has been called "the best kept secret in sports", bocce.

This edition dedicated to our long-time friend and bocce aficionado Del Bracci who passed away at the age of 94. One of the most interesting people from our area, Del was a great athlete, a concert musician, and a fine gentleman. A one-time Super Senior National Downhill Ski Champ, he got to the final heat for the gold medal, competing against two former members of the Romanian Olympic team.

"Those guys were great," he told me in his customary soft spoken voice. With a twinkle in his eye he quickly added "but they had to settle for silver and bronze."

Chapter 1

A Brief History Lesson

B occe is an ancient game, its origin and evolution obscured by the mists of antiquity. The waters are further muddied by the fact that its development is intertwined with that of other bowling games. It is often unclear whether a historical reference refers to lawn bowls, bocce, or bowling. The more I attempted to research the history of bocce, the more I realized that there is no definitive history of the sport. What follows is less a history than a mixture of fact, conjecture, lore, and outright guess (don't look for footnotes and references). The lack of detailed documentation, however, makes the tale no less intriguing.

Sir Flinders Petrie, emeritus professor of Egyptology at the University of London, unearthed an Egyptian tomb from 5200 B.C. bearing evidence of a bowling game played by young boys tossing balls or polished stones. Other Egyptian wall paintings and vases also appear to depict bocce-like games in progress. Some historians have gone as far as to call bocce the ancestor of all ball games.

It is believed that thousands of years ago inhabitants of Pharaoh's Egypt became the first bocce players (must have been a welcome diversion from stacking pyramid stones). Later, Roman legionnaires played with naturally rounded rocks or perhaps coconuts brought back from African campaigns (must have been a welcome diversion from stacking corpses of the conquered). Bocce may have derived from an ancient Greek exercise of throwing balls or stones of varying size for distance. This sound mind, sound body ideal of the Greeks was right up the alley of the Romans, who modified the activity, tossing and rolling the balls along the ground toward a stationary target.

Bocce spread throughout the Middle East and Asia. Historians believe that the Greeks latched onto the game at around 600 B.C. (as evidenced in the painting and sculpture of the period) and introduced it to the Romans. The Romans probably took it on the road via their world conquest and spread the game Johnny Appleseed style. During breaks in the Punic Wars, soldiers selected a small stone "leader" and threw it first. Then they rolled, tossed, or heaved larger stones, with those coming closest to the leader scoring points. All of this appears to have been easy exercise and a pleasant change of pace from the stress of battle.

The Egyptian game became bocce in Italy, and was altered slightly to become boules in France and lawn bowls in England. It is easy to imagine the early games being played with spherical rocks or even coconuts (later, artisans would use hard olive wood to carve out balls). Many (including me) thought the name bocce was derived from the Italian *bacio* meaning kiss. The idea is to kiss, snuggle, or otherwise get close to the object of your affection -- the pallino. Alas! After a New York Times columnist read this in my book and reprinted it, a reader fluent in Italian (writer, editor and Italian tutor Michael P. San Filippo) set us straight.

"...although the article asserts that '...the name of the game, after all, is derived from the Italian word for kiss,' the word has nothing to do with kissing!

In Italian the word for kiss is bacio (from the first-conjugation verb baciare) and the plural is baci. The term bocce is derived from boccia, which in turn gave rise to the verb bocciare (to hit or strike an opponent's ball, causing it to move further away from the pallino, or object ball. The confusion stems from the mispronunciation of the word bocce. Most American English speakers pronounce it BAH-che instead of BOH-chay. There ARE kisses that knock you off your feet, but not in this game!" (visit San Filippo's http://italian.about.com).

When Italian immigrants brought their game to America in the late 19th and early 20th centuries, it was a regionalized version of the activity. Just as there are similar yet somewhat different dialects throughout any country, there were similar yet varying ways of playing bocce. Each area used the regionalized rules from their part of Italy and these changed and evolved over the years. Bocce is and has remained a remarkably resilient game, surviving and growing despite these problems.

In Italy and in the early days of bocce in the United States, women and children were discouraged from playing. This game was the domain of men. It may have begun to die out because men did not share it with women and the younger generation. Its resurgence today is due to the fact that play is no longer confined to adult, Italian males. It has escaped its ethnic roots and has become a game for people of all ages. A movement is on today to construct courts in public parks. This is a major step toward spreading the game to more and more Americans. Extending the game from the private sector (social clubs that require membership fees) to the public sector also provides the opportunity to get outdoors and play in the fresh air with family and friends. In Martinez, California, affiliates of the United States Bocce Federation maintain 15 outdoor courts. You can even get pizza delivered to your "door" by telephoning and specifying your bocce court number.

Played in Italy since before the Caesars, bocce has survived the Fall of the Roman Empire and the threat of fascism. It has evolved to a tournament sport carrying ever-increasing cash prizes and luring corporate sponsors. Undoubtedly it will thrive and continue to flourish. This is testimony to the enduring appeal of an activity that evolved in different parts of the world, is played somewhat differently from country to country, yet whose basic idea is the same. Let's see who can roll, toss, or otherwise deliver their bocce balls closest to the object ball. Bocce, played widely today in Italy, Australia, South America, and other countries, is about to explode in the United States.

Taking the Game on the Road

Jim Vaughan, sales manager extraordinaire for the Bargetto Winery (3535 North Main St., Soquel, CA 95073 – www.bargetto.com) has "taken the game on the road". According to Vaughan, "I introduce Bargetto wines to buyers and wine consumers with bocce as the sporting background. Some of the wine and bocce venues were on the traditional surface, while others were improvised. For instance, we played on the carpet of a French bistro in Singapore, a putting green on the island of Kauai, inside a warehouse in Seattle and alongside horse stables in Tucson. The fusion of wine tasting, food, music and a relaxing (often very competitive) bocce tournament creates an appealing social dynamic."

Bargetto's Cal-Ital signature wine

Vaughan's bocce and wine tasting participants began asking numerous questions about the game (especially about its history). His research lead him to *Storia Delle Bocce In Italia E Nel Mondo* (*The Story of Bocce in Italy and the World*). With the editorial assistance of Bargetto Wine Club Director Ms. Dana Sheldon, Vaughan wrote two newsletters reviewing the first volume of this three-volume masterpiece.

The historical trilogy, published in Italian by Signor Daniele Di Chiara (and thirty years in the making), isn't available for purchase. Di Chiara's effort (as historian for the Federazione Italiana Bocce in Rome, Italy) was primarily for the "love and prosperity of the game."

Vaughan, after having sections of the texts translated into English, reveals that Di Chiara acknowledges the "…murky anecdotal evidence…" that surrounds bocce's origin. Following bocce through time, the author cites more conclusive evidence in the well preserved ruins of Pompeii (destroyed by Mt. Vesuvius in 79 A.D.).

Daniele Di Chiara

STORIA DELLE BOCCE IN ITALIA E NEL MONDO

I

Edizioni Pa.Li.Graf s.r.l. - Pomezia

"Inside one room were nine spherical stones, all perfectly round. One of the stones was considerably smaller, the target ball. This room became known as Bocciodromo (The Bocce Room)."

It is common belief that Greek colonists introduced bocce to the Roman Legions. Di Chiara explains, "The Romans developed a better quality of the game of bocce. They took it from simple manifestation of force to proof of ability. Not a matter of distance but how the stone would make the other one move."

According to Vaughan "The Greeks were shot putting, and the Romans gave it a degree of skill and wit. This version was introduced as the Legions marched, conquered and expanded the Roman Empire. It was not only popular with the soldiers during their free time, but enjoyed by local artists, the noble elite, politicians and the common citizenry.

By the Middle Ages, most European countries were playing some form of bocce (also referred to as 'boules'). To this day, France and England have the closest cousins to bocce: pétanque and lawn bowling."

Vaughan concludes that "Daniele Di Chiara and his team of editors and researchers have truly captured the passionate spirit of the ancient game."

Nailed Boules – Nineteenth Century France

Quite by accident I learned of France's nailed boules, a fascinating part of bocce history. Recently a bocce buddy of mine took me to visit an antique dealer in Salem, Massachusetts.

"Come take a ride" he said. "This dealer has a box of metal bocce balls you might like."

Thinking they might be the small metal pétanque balls, I resisted.

"No," my friend insisted. "These are about the same size as the bocce balls we play with every week."

Reluctantly, I tagged along on this lazy Saturday afternoon. Good thing I did! In a cardboard box underneath some old furniture in the back of this quaint shop in the city of the infamous witch trials were… balls. Not just balls, but hand crafted works of art with what appeared to be individual nails pounded into some kind of wood center. The craftsmanship was fabulous. A couple had numbers on them configured by different colored nails. Two were absolutely beautiful…a kind of mosaic of different color metals.

I purchased the lot of them, took some photos and posted them on my web site, hoping that some reader would enlighten us about what I now had in my possession.

Part of the author's collection

Frank Pipal, a boules (pétanque) player from Sonoma County, California came through with flying colors.

"What you've got is a bunch of very nice Boules Lyonnaises (or volo balls if you like). They are widely collected and desirable - which all the antique dealers in France know. They would have been made in France in the years prior to the appearance of the "Integrale", the first all metal boule.

Nails of copper and brass allow the artisan to create designs.

The author's favorites.

There were many styles of nail work. The core is a ball of boxwood root.

The word bocce, (bocca in Provencal - the language of southern France) comes from the Latin for Boxwood - buxus. The numbers are simply to identify the balls. Often the balls carry the initials of the owner (made to order), or designs.

There's a village in the south of France that is famous for its nailed boules (Aiguines). The trade died out in the thirties with the advent of the Integrale in bronze and then the JB all steel boule.

Aiguines was famous for the small boules used in the Jeu Provencal and later in Pétanque. They are usually "fish-scaled". The big balls were probably made closer to Lyon and Grenoble and other centers of that style of play."

From the Wegner Collection

Besides educating us about this fascinating art, Frank did us a great favor by alerting us to a fabulous web site on the subject.

"What you really need to do is go to Herbert Wegner's web site and see what is probably the most beautiful collection anywhere."

http://perso.wanadoo.fr/herbert.wegner/

WARNING – visit this site at your own risk. If these nailed boules pique your interest, you will likely spend great stretches of time here, keeping you from chores or other tasks (all the more reason to visit).

There are some "must see" pages with spectacular images. The excellent, well-crafted site gives details of the history of this fascinating part of bocce's past. "Different nails" outlines the various nailing techniques. "BOULES" displays images of 80 magnificent nailed boules. "Old pictures+cards" highlights postcard/picture reproductions that positively enthrall.

A Word About Bowls (Lawn Bowling)

"What sport shall we devise here in this garden, to drive away the heavy thought of care?" Queen Isabella queries in Shakespeare's Richard II. "Madam, we'll play at bowls," responds her handmaid. Lawn bowls is a ball-and-target game similar to bocce, in that players roll balls toward a stationary object, but is played on a closely cropped grass lawn without side and end boards. The eight- to ten-ounce jack is rolled down the course and competitors use three-pound bowls made of wood, rubber, or composition material to try to score points. These bowls are not round but biased; they are elliptical and weighted on one side. The weighting was originally accomplished by loading the ball with lead, but now is done by making one side more convex than the other. When rolled, this bias causes the ball to curve like a ten-pin bowling ball (perhaps lawn bowls is the precursor of that game). An interesting wrinkle to this game is that as each ball is delivered, the player's rear foot must be on, or above, a small, strategically placed mat.

New York's Bowling Green is a reminder that bowls was an important recreation for early settlers. George Washington's dad built a bowling green at Mt. Vernon in 1732, and the game enjoyed great popularity until the Revolutionary War, after which it became dormant for the next 100 years or so. George Vanderbilt and John D. Rockefeller had private bowling greens on their estates, and Walt Disney hosted bowling friends at his Palm Springs home.

A Word About Boules (Pétanque)

Boules, jeu de boules, or pétanque are names for the French version of bowls or bocce. Although the game is played in many countries, boules is as closely associated with France as bullfighting is with Spain. It is usually played on sand or gravel with metal balls that are smaller than bocce or lawn bowls. Like bowls, the game is played without side or end boards on an area called a *pitch*. The object ball (beut or cochonnet) is so small (on the order of a table tennis ball) that the game is difficult to play on grass. Even closely cropped lawns tend to obliterate it from view. As in lawn bowls, the rules require players to take their shots from a designated area (often both feet within a circle drawn or painted on the ground).

Kissing the Fanny

Pétanque, it appears, is responsible for the tradition whereby losing bocce or boules teams are obliged to "kiss the fanny." Kissing fanny is the punishment for losing a game without scoring a single point. ALL players defeated by a shut-out have to kiss the fanny with the winning team serving as witnesses. This is why, wherever boules is played, a figure of a fake fanny is fervidly flaunted. Whether a painting, picture or ceramic sculpture, the unhappy losers are obliged to peck, in public, the usually generous cheeks of the image.

Legend has it that the tradition started in France's Savoy region. The first Fanny (a common first name in France) was a waitress at the Café de Grand-Lemps,

Photograph courtesy of Playaboule.com

circa World War I. A gentle and compassionate soul, she would allow customers who had lost at boules without scoring a solitary point to kiss her on the cheek.

One day it was the village mayor who had been "skunked" and came to collect his kiss. Reportedly, there was "bad blood" between the two, and intending to humiliate the mayor, Fanny stepped up onto a chair, lifted her skirt and offered him... her fanny! The mayor was up to the challenge and, two loud kisses echoed through the café...the beginning of a longstanding tradition...

A Classic Case of One-Upmanship

The three ball-and-target games of bocce, boules, and bowls are classic contests of one-upmanship. If you can roll the ball six inches away from the target, I can draw to within five. Such activities have had enormous appeal, especially when the elements of strategy and team competition are added to the mix. And 7000 years of staying power is a pretty good endorsement. If we consider bocce, boules, and bowls variations of the same game, that game must be classified as one of the largest participatory sports in the world today.

CHAPTER 2

THE GAME

B occe is a simple yet elegant game. Although I love the game as it is played in courts across the country and throughout the world, I'm partial to the simplified, backyard version - the one that can be played by men and women, boys and girls of almost any age. This game can be learned in minutes and played almost anywhere.

Bocce's Appeal

I am an unabashed promoter of bocce. I bring a set of bocce balls along whenever I travel or attend outdoor parties. Starting a game with family or friends on a patch of grass or dirt, we invariably draw a crowd. Inquiring people want to know - how do you play? - What's the object? Are the balls just like bowling balls? Can I hold one to see how heavy it is? Most often they've heard of bocce, but have seldom, if ever, played. After a three-minute explanation and a quick try, they're hooked. They want to know where to get their hands on a set of bocce balls and, chances are good that they'll become bocce buffs.

Played the way we'll describe here, bocce is a gentle pastime, an entertaining recreational endeavor. Females should be pleased that in this age of male dominated sports, bocce is suited equally to both sexes. Co-ed games are not only possible, but desirable. The tendency with backyard bocce is to include everyone - husbands and wives, neighbors, children - all want the ball in their court.

In subsequent chapters we'll take you through the terminology, examine the strategy, and tell you where to get equipment. We'll even describe how to construct a court of your own (if you have the inclination and the place to build one). But for now, here are the basics - enough for you to begin playing today.

Getting Down to Basics

A set of bocce balls consists of eight large balls and one small ball called the pallino (Italian for little ball). The larger balls are roughly the size of a grapefruit (the size, weight and composition vary with manufacturers and some offer a variety of sizes and weights to suit the individual player - see Chapter 6 - The Equipment). Two teams compete against each other in this ball-and-target game. Each team gets to roll or otherwise toss four of the larger balls toward the pallino (also called the jack, pill, or object ball). Each team's four bocce balls are of a different color or are otherwise marked for differentiation. For example, a set might consist of four red balls, four green balls and a yellow or white pallino.

The object of the game is to score points by getting your team's balls close to the pallino. Novices think it advantageous to hit the pallino, but this may or may not be true. In any case, you don't score by hitting the pallino, but by directing your bocce balls closer to it than your opponents can. After both teams roll all of their balls, the frame or round is completed, and only one team will score. You score one point for each ball that is closer to the pallino than the closest ball of your opponent (to the pallino). Score one point if your ball is closest to the pallino, two points if you have the two closest to the pallino, etc. In this way, you can score up to four points in each frame.

The game can continue to 11, 12, 15, 16 or even 21 points (or another score that is mutually acceptable to the participants). We suggest games of 12 and that score is pretty standard in the USA. This is sufficiently long to make for fair competition, yet doesn't keep the on-deck players waiting too long (there are always on-deck players). Some tournament directors schedule games to 12 but increase the winning score to 15 or 16 in the finals, presumably to ensure that the better team wins. (The shorter the game, the better the chance of an upset.)

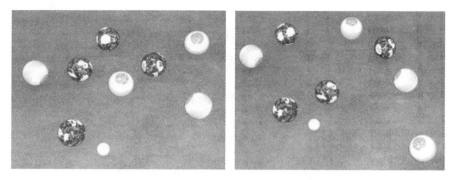

One point   Two points

One point   Two points

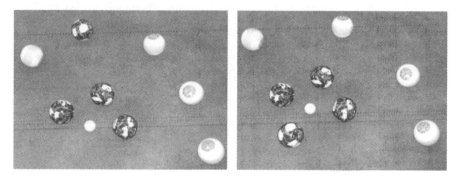

Three points   Four points

In lawn bowls they sometimes play a set number of "ends" (frames or rounds) instead of playing to a set point total. They might agree, for example, that the leader after 15 ends is the victor.

An elderly woman from Florida told me that her group played games to 21. "Wow!" I said. "Those games must take forever."

"Well," she countered, "We have a lot of time at the senior center."

Although not very common, we sometimes hear of areas where they play "deuce game" – the winner must win by two points. Rick Bushong, webmaster for the Crockett Bocce Club (California) web site says that "the two point rule makes for some exciting finishes in close games."

Note: Although there are variations to the rules played around the country, a serious attempt to establish a standard set of "open" or "recreational" rules has been made by many groups. Of course, these rules have differed slightly (and sometimes not so slightly) from group to group. Rules for international bocce play are well established, having been used worldwide for years. These will govern any future Olympic games, and are far more disciplined and complicated than the recreational rules discussed here (see Chapter 11 for international rules). In an effort to standardize what we call Open Rules (as opposed to the international rules) the United States Bocce Federation has sanctioned the USBF Open Rules which I have reprinted in Chapter 10.

The game is best played with one to four players per team. In the one-on-one version (singles), each player rolls four balls. With two players per team (doubles) each participant tosses two balls. And the four vs. four game allows one shot for each team member. This last method of play has its ups and downs. On the plus side, it involves eight players at once. On the negative side, you only get one shot per frame (you do more watching than playing), and this prevents you from getting a feel for the terrain on any given lie.

With four-player teams there are two different formats. You can roll one ball each, as described earlier, with all eight players playing from the same starting location. After the frame or round, the eight players walk to the other end of the court or play area and begin play back in the opposite direction. Of course, in your backyard or playground area (sans court) you can play in any direction you choose. We prefer to roll the pallino right from where we just completed the round, rather than picking up the balls and moving to a new starting point.

The alternate format is to station four participants (two from each team) at either end of your play area. With this method, each participant tosses two balls and stays at his end. We are basically dividing the teams of four into two subgroups of two. When the group from one end plays, the other group members act as coaches, fans, and most importantly - measurers. We keep a cumulative score - if you score two points and then your partners score two points, you are ahead four to nothing. Critics of this style claim that "you are only playing half a game" and "it reduces the exercise (walking) that bocce provides."

Two-on-two (doubles) is my favorite way to play bocce. You get two shots, allowing you to "go to school" on your first ball, and you get a partner allowing for greater camaraderie. After each frame you walk to the other end, pick up the balls and begin play in another direction.

You can also play with three players per team (triples). You have to decide who on each team will get the extra ball each frame (two of the three partners roll one ball while the third gets to roll two). Perhaps you could rotate it. You could even keep the six active by stationing four players at one end (two bocce balls each) and two at the other (four balls each). But with six or more players I prefer teams of two in a kind of round robin format. Play games of 12 and have the on-deck team have a burger or act as measurers or referees. Depending on the skill of the participants, games last anywhere from 15 to 45 minutes.

Another option with three-player teams is to add another half set of balls (2 more red and two more green) so that each player can deliver two balls. All six players roll two balls each and walk back and forth playing both ends of the court. Three-player teams would require 6 balls per team (12 balls in play), so, theoretically a team could score six points in one round.

To begin the game, teams must agree on who will toss the pallino first. You might flip a coin, throw fingers in the old odds-evens game of our youth, or come up with another alternative. The game starts when one player tosses the pallino to any position he desires. In our backyard bocce version there is no minimum or maximum distance that the pallino must be tossed (unless the players agree to such restrictions beforehand). Now the person who tossed the pallino tosses the first bocce ball, attempting to get as close to the pallino as possible. While you don't get points for hitting the object ball, a shot that nestles right up to pallino, obscuring it from the next player's sight, is very tough to beat. In any case, once the first ball is played, that team has the advantage - they're closest. Now it is up to the opponents to roll their bocce balls until they win the point - by getting closest to the pallino - so far. This may take one, two, three, or all four balls. Play continues in this manner (sometimes referred to as the nearest ball rule) until all balls are played and one team scores one, two, three, or four points. To recap - when Team A has the point (has the closest ball, or is "in"), they step aside and wait until Team B beats that point (has the "in" ball). Team B rolls as many balls as needed to "out-lag" Team A's ball. If they can do it with one ball, fine. Now they will "hold the point" as some players say, and Team A has to try to beat Team B's point. Obviously, a good first shot could force the opponents to use two, three, or even all four of their balls. This puts the team with a good first "pointer" in an advantageous position.

Note: after the initial toss of the coin and subsequent first round of play, the team that scores always rolls the pallino. Also, the team rolling the pallino must play the first ball as well. Teammates may decide among themselves who will toss the pallino, or they may alternate this privilege, but the honor must go to someone on the team that scored.

Sometimes a shot is so close that it is too difficult to out-lag. In this case a team is likely to try to knock it away with either a fast rolling shot called a *raffa* or a direct hit on the fly called a *volo*. In either case, successfully knocking away a close ball opens up the play for you or your teammate to come in for the point. As you will see in subsequent chapters, this movement of opponents' balls, your own team's balls, or even the pallino, makes for an infinite variety of possible tactics.

Order of Play Within a Team

In singles play each player tosses four balls, so play proceeds quite simply. If your opponent is "in", it's your shot next. But with two or more players per team you need to decide which player will roll when your opponents have the point. You might agree ahead of time that "I'll throw the first two balls and you throw the last two." In four-person teams (one ball to be played by each) you can also preset the order by designating a first, second, third, and fourth shooter. But most often teams will discuss strategy while the game is in progress and agree, "You are better at this type of shot - why don't you try it?" The only restriction is that whichever team has the point (has the nearest ball) - a player from the other team must play next.

On bocce courts, lines are marked to indicate how far forward a player may stand when rolling a ball. Since courts are lined by sideboards, this limits players' lateral movement. But there are no such restrictions in an open backyard. Usually this doesn't present a problem - players agree to take their shots from the same general area. Sometimes disagreements arise when a number of balls are in front of the object ball and the shooter doesn't have a clear view of it. He takes a step to his right. Then another. And another. Clearly there has to be some limit or he could circle completely around to the other side of the balls. Try to get everybody to play from a couple steps left or right of the spot from where the object ball was rolled into play. If this doesn't work out, put down a welcome mat and instruct all to place one foot on the rug when taking their shots.

The Playing Surface

Although bocce is played worldwide on enclosed clay, stone dust or synthetic courts, you can play on almost any surface. You need only a dirt or grassy area of 30 to 70 feet long by at least eight feet in width. It may be perfectly level, extremely hilly, or anywhere in between. In fact, sloping areas on the playing field make for interesting shots involving "reading the green" as in golf. Generally, good golfers (especially good putters) make good bocce players. They're skilled at gauging just how far a ball might break to the right or left and they tend to have a soft touch (smooth release of the ball). Basketball players with good shooting touch also tend to make fine bocce players. They know how to let the ball roll off the fingertips imparting a forward spin to the ball (12 o'clock to 6 o'clock rotation). In contrast, we often encounter very good players who have never participated in traditional sports.

Just as the enclosed court introduces a dimension of playing off the side and end boards, playing on the green (or dirt) adds a nifty element. You can toss the object ball in one direction, play a round, and then proceed in any other direction. You might roll the pallino near the base of that willow tree and see if you can navigate over, around, or through the exposed roots. Or you could place it near that chain link fence (acting as a kind of sideboard) and try to carom shots, first kissing the ball off the fence, then steering it neatly next to the object ball. The possibilities are endless.

In backyard lawn bocce, most people play a kind of anything-goes style. One player told me about spirited games played at family cookouts. In one particularly competitive contest the pallino got bounced up into the air and landed right in a trash can. One family member, acting as referee, offered… "I'll get the pallino out of the trash and we'll start the frame over." This was met by a chorus of "Like hell you will!" Both teams then attempted to gain the point by tossing balls into the barrel on the fly.

Measuring for Point

Measuring to find out which ball is closest to the pallino can present problems. At the most noncompetitive level of recreational bocce, players often concede a point on a close call or just agree to call it a tie (no point scored). At the opposite end of the spectrum, participants use state-of-the-art measuring devices complete with calipers capable of discerning fractions of an inch.

The first rule in determining the nearest ball is to move up to the area of the pallino. Sometimes a ball that appears to be inches away when viewed from the foul line is actually several feet away when viewed up close. And the angle can fool you. For example, Team A's first roll may end up about even with, but a foot or two to the right of the pallino. Team B's shot is straight on, but apparently six inches or so short of the pallino. Before Team A plays the next ball, they should get a better look by walking up to the balls and surveying the situation. Quite often the ball that appears to be six inches short is actually several feet short. Of course, this trip to the pallino is unnecessary if you have someone acting as referee.

| From the end that the shot originates from it might appear that the ball in front is IN... | But, from the proper viewing angle you can better see that the other ball is actually closer to the target. |

A second important rule for determining which ball is IN, is to stand behind the object in a kind of straddling position with the balls that are in contention in clear view (see photos). Experienced players can determine which ball is in for the point even when one ball is only a fraction of an inch closer than another.

Good position for the observer to call a point by eye

My family and I have enjoyed backyard bocce for many years measuring only by eye or with feet, hands, and fingers. This nifty system really works! Start at the pallino and place the heel of your foot against it. Take care not to displace the pallino. Take "baby steps" straight toward the ball you are measuring, carefully placing the heel of one foot directly in front of the toe of the previous. When you get too close to the bocce ball to squeeze in another foot, keep your front foot in place, and bending down, use your fingers as more precise units of measure. In this way we can tell that the ball that is three feet and four fingers away is "out", and the one that is three feet and three fingers away is "in".

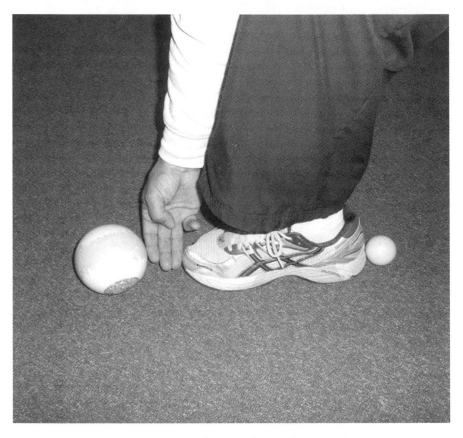

One foot + 3 fingers from the target

When the distances to be measured are smaller than feet and awkward for fingers, or require a bit more precision, we have used twigs, pieces of string, and other easily accessible objects. A telescoping radio, television, or car antenna works very well if it is sturdy and straight. A standard tape measure is helpful, especially for very long measurements. We have seen some neat homemade measurers, too. One creative guy on the bocce circuit taped a car antenna and a presentation pointer together so that they could be opened telescopically in opposite directions. "A single antenna is good" he claims, "but it's just not long enough for many measurements." Finally, there are some precise measuring devices on the market which we outline in Chapter 6, The Equipment.

Some Pointers on Measuring for Point

1. Stand by the pallino and see if you can make the call by eye. Give opponents a peek and see if you can come to an agreement.

2. Be extremely careful not to displace the pallino or bocce balls during measuring. If you do move a ball and cannot agree on its placement, it is good form to award the point to the team not responsible for the accidental movement. Some players like to secure the object ball's position by pressing down on it during measurement. This might be okay for informal play, but no one should touch any balls during measurement. It only increases the chance that you will inadvertently move a ball.

3. To score a point, a ball has to be closer to the pallino than the other team's ball. A tie just doesn't cut it. If, when the frame is completed, you determine that the closest balls rolled by Team A and Team B are tied (equal distance from the pallino), no points are scored. These balls do not cancel each other out and make the next closest ball a point. Again, no points may be scored when the two closest balls are from opposite teams and are equidistant from the object ball.

4. If one, two, or three points are sure, and two opposing team's balls are the next closest to pallino and tied, the previously determined points are scored, but the tied balls mean nothing.

5. Tape measurements (metric units are always preferable to English) are sometimes made from the bocce ball to the center of the pallino (or vice versa). Instruct one person to place the end of the tape measure at the middle (equator) of the bocce ball, and direct another to extend the tape over the top center of the pallino and to read the result (or the other way around – pallino to top center of bocce ball being measured). This method requires a little estimation on the part of the measurer in terms of interpreting just where the center of the pallino is. The method is adequate, but can cause problems when two measurements are very close. Some players prefer to measure from the outer dimensions of the balls, but the best and most accurate way to determine which ball is IN is with *inside measure*. You want to know which ball has the smaller amount of space between it and the pallino. Hold the tape measure or other

device in between the two balls, measuring from the middle (equator) of one to the middle of the other. Then move to the other ball in contention and compare your two findings.

For long measures, a standard tape measure can be used. Often one player holds the tape's end at the pallino and the other estimates the distance over the top center of the ball being measured.

Inside measure is the most accurate. Here the Premier Boule Measure is put to good use.

Play Ball!

Now you know enough to play bocce. Give it a shot and come back and read some more later. In some rounds you may have difficulty telling which ball is closest to the object ball. Remember to get the best angle for determining which ball is IN by standing by the object ball. If you cannot make the call by eye, you will have to resort to a measurement. In subsequent chapters, we'll take you deeper into the strategy and finer points of play. For now, you know enough to go out and enjoy this great and ancient game.

A Dozen Steps to the Joy of Bocce

1. Secure a set of bocce balls, a place to play, and some players.
2. Make two equal teams. One-, two-, three- or four-person teams are most common.
3. Toss a coin or otherwise select who will play first.

4. The team that wins the coin toss pitches the pallino and then rolls the first bocce ball, trying to draw as near as possible to the pallino.

5. The starting team stands aside and does not bowl again until the opposing team gets one of their bocce balls closer to the pallino or runs out of bocce balls.

6. Play proceeds in this manner, observing the "nearest ball rule". The team with the nearest ball stands aside and waits until such time that the other team has the nearest ball or has used up all its balls in the attempt. Remember – the team that is OUT *plays* – the team that is IN *delays*.

7. After both teams deliver all their balls, the frame or round is over. Score one point for each ball that is closer to the pallino than the closest ball of your opponent.

8. The team that scores the point(s) starts the next frame by rolling the pallino and the first bocce ball.

9. Games can be played to any mutually agreeable count. USBF Open Rules call for games of at least 12 points.

10. Balls can be tossed underhand or overhand, through the air or bowled along the ground.

11. Think ahead – like chess. Possible strategies include knocking an opponent's ball out of scoring position, redirecting the pallino to a new position, and leaving a ball in front of the pallino to block your opponent's attempt.

12. Have fun with this wonderful and ancient pastime – the best kept secret in sports.

Play on grass on hilly
or level terrain

Play on the beach at low tide

Play at the beach at high tide

Play in the snow

Play on your backyard court or
on courts in the public domain

Play on courts at private clubs

The Joy of Bocce

CHAPTER 3

THE TERMINOLOGY

The terms that follow are listed alphabetically. Rather than a technical glossary, this section is designed in an easy-to-read format. It will familiarize the reader with words and situations that are used throughout the rest of the text. A brief perusal of these terms will set the stage for a clearer understanding of the chapters that follow. From *bank shot* to *winning score*, this sampling of bocce jargon will get you rolling in the right direction. Keep in mind that there is a difference between the way the game is played in recreational and tournament settings and the way it is played in international competition.

bank shot – when playing on courts complete with side and backboards, a shot caromed off the side and/or backboard (illegal in international play).

bocce – can refer to the balls used in the game or the game itself (e.g. players roll their bocce balls while enjoying a game of bocce). The balls can be made of wood, plastic, or composite material. Each of the eight balls in a set is four to five inches in diameter and weighs about two pounds. One team's balls are distinguished from another's by color (e.g. four green balls, four red balls, and a smaller object ball or pallino of another color). In some sets, balls of the same color are inscribed with distinctive engraving so that teammates' balls can be differentiated from each other. In international volo play the balls are metallic (often an alloy like bronze). Note: As stated earlier, the word bocce means the game and the implement used to play the game (much like baseball refers to the ball and the game). Purists don't refer to the game as bocce ball. It is improper to ask "Do you want to play bocce ball?" or "Are you entered in the bocce ball tournament?"

"Do you want to play bocce?" and "Are you entered in the bocce tournament?" represent accepted usage. The word is also commonly used in this manner: "Roll your bocce off the sideboard."

Perfetta Club Pro bocce set with carry bag by Playaboule

Dr. Angelo Cordano, one of the top Italian-American players, gives us this lesson to clarify the Italian...

"**Boccia** is a single ball (UNA / ONE ball)

Boccie is the PLURAL – e.g., six boccie

and **Bocce** is the GAME we like."

bocce court or **bocce alley** (sometimes called the **campo**, occasionally **pit**, but this is more properly used for horseshoes) – the enclosed playing surface complete with side and end boards. The surface may be a fine gravel, clay, stone dust, crushed limestone, or oyster flour. Occasionally, court surfaces are grass, indoor/outdoor carpet or other artificial material. Courts are generally 60 to 90 feet in length (almost 90 feet for international competition). Sixty-foot courts (common in the east) are a tad short for serious players. Seventy to 76 feet seems to be a fair compromise between 60' and 90'. Ten to twelve feet in width is acceptable. Sideboards should be at least as high as the balls (eight to twelve inches recommended) and often higher at both ends where high velocity shots are more likely to knock the pallino out of the play-

ing area. The United States Bocce Federation strongly recommends international size courts (approximately 88' by 13'). These dimensions provide a court suitable for international rules as well as for open recreational rules. See Chapter 8, Building a Backyard Court, for more details on court dimensions and construction.

Bocce court at the home of Eric Marttila—Doylestown, Pennsylvania

boules – the French word for the balls and their version of the game – also called pétanque. The balls are metallic and much smaller and lighter than bocce balls. The object ball (*but* or *cochonnet*) is significantly smaller, too (on the order of a table tennis ball). The game of boules is played on dirt or gravel without side or end boards. It is difficult to play on grass because even closely cropped lawns are likely to obscure the tiny object ball. The game is very similar to bocce and it is not much of a stretch to accept that bocce, boules, and lawn bowling all had a common ancestor.

bowls – the English game of lawn bowling and the balls themselves. The balls are biased (weighted on one side) so curving shots are common. The name bocce is sometimes used interchangeably with lawn bowling but, despite their similarities, they are two different games.

court markings – when playing on an enclosed court, as opposed to a patch of grass or dirt, the court has lines as prescribed by rule (regulations may vary from area to area). For this discussion, let's assume a 76-foot court. To begin a frame, the pallino must cross the half court mark which is 38 feet from the end. A pallino toss short of this line must be picked up and rolled again. Some rules mandate a line at each end of the court, four feet from the back or end board across which the pallino may not pass on the initial toss. While play progresses, the position of the pallino may change by being hit by another ball (intentionally or accidentally). It may come to rest beyond the 72-foot line, but it may never end up closer to the players than midcourt, or the frame is dead and must be played over. (In addition, some rules call for the pallino to come to rest a minimum distance from the side boards – usually 12 inches)

dead ball – a disqualified ball. In outdoor, recreational bocce using "open rules," there is almost never a dead ball. In club and tournament play on enclosed courts, a ball may be disqualified if:

- there is a penalty such as a foot foul
- it leaves the court's playing surface
- it comes into contact with a person or object outside the court
- it hits the top of the court boards
- it hits the covering of the courts or any supports

doubles – the game of bocce played with partners (two against two). Each player rolls two balls.

end – see **frame**.

end boards – on a court, the backboards at each end. Players often carom shots off the side and end boards attempting to score points, although international rules prohibit play off the side and end boards.

Rather than just a static backboard, most courts have an additional swinging or hanging board that serves to absorb the force of a hard shot, preventing a rebound. The facing of these swinging boards is often covered with an absorbent material (carpeting, fire hose, rubber tubing, etc.). On long shots, this prevents a player from getting close to the pallino simply by smacking the end board and relying on the rebound effect to bring the ball into scoring position. Rather, a more skillful shot involving smooth touch and release is required.

foul line – on enclosed courts the foul line is the line the player must stand behind when rolling his bocce ball. Many players move forward toward the target as they release the ball to improve accuracy The ball must be released before the player passes the foul line. Some rules specify two foul lines – especially for play on shorter courts. For example, many 60-foot courts have a pointing line four feet from each end and a shooting or hitting line nine feet from each end. Many players take several steps in their approach when trying to hit a ball away. This would not be possible without a longer runway. On the other hand, this longer runway would bring the player too close to his target while attempting to close in for a point, so he would have to deliver his ball from behind the four-foot line when pointing. Some groups who play on longer courts approve one foul line for both pointing and hitting, reasoning that the greater distance makes the pointing line unnecessary.

| Sometimes the foul line is painted on the sideboards. | Sometimes the foul line is marked on the court surface. |

fouls – (also foot fouls, foot line fouls) – violations of the rules caused by a player stepping over the pointing line or hitting line before the ball leaves the player's hand. Players may not step over the foremost part of the line with any part of the foot before the ball leaves the hand. Some sets of rules call for one warning on a foot foul. Subsequent fouls carry penalties. When playing international rules you may step on but not completely over the foul line when pointing.

frame – also end or round; The period of time during which players from both teams roll their bocce balls from one end of the court to the other and points are awarded – similar to an inning in baseball or softball. When points are tallied, the frame is completed. If Team A scores one point each frame and the winning score is twelve, the contest will last twelve frames. Unlike softball or baseball, with games of seven or nine innings, the number of frames played in bocce is not predetermined.

hitting – (see also **raffa**) – Rolling the ball with great force to displace a ball or balls, also shooting, spocking, hitting. Since players often use a two-, three-, or four-step delivery for this shot, they may advance to the second foul line (hitting or spocking line) for this shot (assuming the court uses separate lines for pointing and hitting). The ball must be released before the foot crosses the foul line.

initial point – the first ball thrown toward the object ball becomes the "IN" ball and establishes the initial point. It is always incumbent on the team with pallino advantage to establish the initial point.

in – the ball closest to the pallino. "Our team's ball is 'IN' so your team must play the next ball." Some say "This red ball is *holding* the point."

lag – also point; to roll for point. To deliver the bocce ball as close to the pallino as possible.

live ball – any ball that has a possibility of scoring a point. Any legally played ball that is resting on the court or in motion as the result of being hit by another live ball. Also, any ball still in the possession of a participant waiting to play.

measuring devices – feet, hands, fingers, twigs, string, tape measures, television antennas, or more specialized implements for determining who has the point.

nearest ball rule – accepted order of play whereby the team with the ball nearest to the object ball stands aside and allows the other team to bowl until they establish the nearest ball (or they run out of balls in the attempt). The obligation to deliver the next ball always belongs to the team that is "OUT", or "AWAY". The same team may roll two, three, even four balls in succession if they cannot out-lag or knock away the other team's point while attempting to establish the "IN" ball.

open rules – a less structured type of play unencumbered by the stringent regulations of international play. Open rules usually govern backyard play as well as a good deal of league and tournament competition. See Chapter 10, Tournament Play & USBF Open Rules.

out – not closest to the pallino. "Your team's ball is IN. Our team's ball is OUT, so it's our turn to roll."

pallino – also called the pallina, object ball, jack, pill. A ball that is smaller than the bocce balls (generally 1 ½ to 2 inches in diameter as opposed to 4 ¼ inches for the larger bocce balls) that is the target in the game of bocce. In a true contest of one-upmanship, teams vie to score points by directing their balls closer to this ball than the opposition can. The pallino, bocce's bull's eye, is always of a color visibly distinct from both teams' bocce balls.

pallino advantage – the favorable position of possessing control of the object ball. The team with pallino advantage gets to roll the pallino to any legal position and must also play the first bocce ball in the round. Pallino advantage is established at the beginning of the game by coin toss (or choosing up, or some other mutually agreeable method) and subsequently goes in each round to the team that scores/wins the round.

pétanque – see **boules**

pointing – also lagging; rolling the bocce ball in an effort to "close in" or draw near the pallino. This is a finesse shot requiring deft touch and smooth release of the ball. It is an attempt to get as close as possible to the object ball – to score a point. Sometimes this is referred to as the punto method. If there are separate foul lines for pointing and hitting, players must use the pointing line for this shot. Those skilled at pointing are considered good pointers or laggers.

punto – smooth roll for point. See **pointing.**

raffa – (see also **hitting**) – a fast rolling shot intended to knock an opponent's ball away or to drive the pallino to a new position. Striking its target on the roll, this smash shot is referred to as hitting, spocking, or popping. Raffa shots usually include a two-, three-, or four-step approach reminiscent of tenpin bowling. Although a raffa in recreational play is usually rolled like a bowler trying for a strike, a true international raffa must be lofted beyond the raffa line, which is three meters in front of the pointing or lagging line.

round – same as frame.

rule of advantage – the option given to a team when opponents have committed an infraction. The option is to accept the result of the illegal play or to remove the illegally delivered ball and return all displaced balls to their previous positions.

selling the point – colorful expression used when a player inadvertently gives the point to his opponent by 1) knocking his own ball out of contention, 2) bumping the opponent's ball into scoring position or 3) redirecting the pallino away from his team's ball(s) or toward the other team's ball(s). "I'm so angry at myself. I sold the point!"

sideboards – on enclosed rectangular courts, a continuous railing of ten- to twelve-inch high wood planking (often pressure treated) that serves to keep bocce balls on the court and in play.

singles – the game of bocce played one-on-one with each player rolling four balls. Sometimes referred to as testa/testa (head to head).

spock – to hit a ball with great force to displace its position. Derived from the Italian spaccare, to break. Americanized, the term is generally used as a verb, "I'll try to spock the ball that's closest to the pallino." Players may advance to the spock line when attempting this shot. See **hitting.**

spock line – also hitting line; on official courts, the line over which a player attempting to hit or spock may not pass until the ball has left the hand.

standing hitter – a player who attempts to hit without taking an approach. Remaining stationary, the player releases a raffa or volo shot. Though they use no approach steps, these players are entitled to advance to the hitting line.

swingboard – See **end boards**.

testa/testa – See **singles**.

triples – a three versus three bocce match. Each player rolls two balls, so twelve bocce balls are in play.

United States Bocce Federation (USBF) – the governing body of bocce in America (www.bocce.com). The USBF is a member of the Federation International de Boules and the Confederazione Boccistica Internazionale.

volo – an aerial shot to knock an opponent's ball out of scoring position or displace the pallino. Skilled players need to approach an 80% to 90% success rate on these airborne knock-away attempts. Some tournament events hold shoot-outs (like the NBA three-point shoot-out) where players compete in a voloing exhibition. Target balls are placed at different locations on the court, some behind other balls adding to the difficulty, and players try to take the volo title by scoring the greatest number of hits.

winning score – bocce games may be played to any predetermined count. Winning totals of 11, 12, 15, and 16 are common while 12 is probably most common in the USA. Unlike some other sports, you don't have to win by two points. The team to first reach the agreed upon score wins the game.

Random Thoughts on Bocce Jargon

One of the things that fascinate me about bocce is not only the variation of play in pockets across the country, but also the jargon that has evolved in different locations. It bugs me to no end when someone asks, "Want to play some bocce ball?" I think of a kid going to the hockey rink or frozen pond and asking his friends if they want to play some "hockey puck." Although American bocce is still struggling to standardize, we should at least agree to call the game "bocce", and reserve "bocce ball" for the round object we roll in the direction of the pallino.

Some refer to the object ball in the masculine (pallino) while others in the feminine (pallina). I also hear jack, kitty, pill, cue ball, mark, and every variation beginning with the letter P from Pauline to piñata.

Hitting an opponent's ball to displace it because it is "in" for a point is one of the nifty skill shots in bocce. If it happens to be a red ball that has the point, I've heard talk about making a shot called a "Visine" – one that's designed to "get the red out!"

And I've heard of closing in for point referred to as "coodling in."

"You have about two feet to work with – coodle right in here for the point."

On the south side of Chicago they "toots it up" when they tap a ball gently to push it closer to the pallino to score the point. A player might counsel his partner with "Roll gently and toots our ball up a little." Therefore, this could logically be called a "tootsie roll."

In some areas, hitting a previously played ball a little closer to the pallino is "bucking it up."

"If you can buck this red ball up a couple inches, it will be in."

Scoring four points in one frame is sometimes referred to as a "four-bagger," like a homerun in baseball. When a team gets all four points in a frame with a neat cluster around the object ball, players from the Long Island Bocce Club call that "four on the floor" or a "casino." To them, pallino advantage is "pallino power" or "power of the pallino".

In Massachusetts players talk about "running the rail" for bank shots or rolls that hug the sideboards.

A ball that is "in" is referred to as "holding point."

"This green ball is holding the point right now," a player might advise his teammate.

The term "cover" means two things – get the point, or block the opponents' path to the pallino.

"You only need to get a ball within three feet to cover" (win the point for your team).

"Cover up by leaving a ball right in front" (leave a ball short to block).

Columbus, Georgia backyard court of Joe Sandri.
The 60' by 12' court is surfaced with pulverized granite.

CHAPTER 4

THE GAME, A CLOSER LOOK

Now that you have read about and played a little bocce, let's take a closer look at the ancient pastime. When Italian immigrants at the turn of the century landed at Ellis Island, bocce passed through customs too. Once in America, Italians tended to keep the game to themselves, playing in backyards and at their social clubs. For many, it was a way of hanging on to the old country – a nostalgic glimpse of their native land. From the outset it was an Italian's diversion, and it was distinctively an Italian *man's* sport. Bocce's recent resurgence is largely due to the fact that non-Italians, young players and women have embraced the game. The increasing number of courts constructed in public parks is also promoting the sport's growth. Today, parents who want to share the game with their children don't have to spend the afternoon at a social club. They can get outside and enjoy the game and the outdoors. While Italians still seem to be the most zealous advocates of bocce (and very good players), they now share the fun with others. Anyone can play, regardless of age, strength or physical condition. If you can roll a ball about the size and weight of a candlepin bowling ball, you can play. Bocce has truly become a game for all people. Having moved slowly but steadily away from its ethnic and male dominated upbringing, bocce is reaching the mainstream.

Still, we promoters of this great game have a way to go. Sometimes referred to as the "best kept secret in sports," there is still a segment of the North American population that has no knowledge of the game. Radio talk show hosts continue to ask me "How do you play?" and "What is the object?" And callers to the radio station ask if bocce is similar to shuffleboard, lawn bowls, and boules. Most obvious is that bocce still suffers from an "image problem". People envision cranky old coots smoking cigars and drinking wine while engaged in "geriatric lawn bowling". And the tone of voice and demeanor of the talk show hosts often reveals their sense that bocce is not really to be taken seriously. While talking bocce on CSRB in Toronto (the largest talk radio show in Canada) the sports director chimed in with "Hey Mario, is there any checking in bocce?"

While those of us promoting this wonderful sport still have our work cut out for us, the up side is that virtually everyone we introduce the game to enjoys it.

Quite similar to the French game of boules or pétanque and the English game of lawn bowls, bocce has subtle differences. Pétanque uses small metal balls that are lofted in an underhand, palm down fashion. And while some use the term bocce as a synonym for lawn bowling, the two are different games. Lawn bowls are large, biased balls which curve or hook during their path to the target. In the United States, bocce is more widely played than lawn bowls and boules. But when grouped together, the three ball-and-target games stand with soccer and golf as three of the largest participatory sports in the world.

Bocce's Attraction Today

Formal bocce is played on courts of hard, compacted clay, stone dust or oyster shell with round, unbiased balls four to five inches in diameter and weighing about two pounds. Singles, doubles, triples, and games with foursomes are popular with little variation in the rules. Bocce requires good judgment of distance and the ability to size up a situation and determine what type of shot or strategy is called for. An eye for analyzing the contour and rough spots or divots on a playing surface is helpful, too. Some bocce players claim that the sport improves their golf, bowling, shuffleboard and horseshoes play since it has features of all these games. In one way, the game is like slow-pitch softball. The slow-pitch delivery, with its six- to twelve-foot arc, is easy to hit, but not that easy to hit well. Similarly, bocce is easy to play, but not that easy to play well. "Although an easy game to learn," comments Phil Ferrari, president of the World Bocce Association, "bocce takes a lifetime to master."

Played widely in the United States both as an organized sport and as informal recreation, part of bocce's attraction is that it can be learned in minutes. Another plus is that the subtle nuances and strategies of play are endless. People learn how to play quickly, since the open rules are easily understood, but they continue learning as long as they compete. Equipment costs are minimal, and maintenance expense is minimal, which makes bocce doubly attractive in this era of budgetary restraint. Though there exists a wide range of specialized bocce shoes, clothing and exotic measuring devices, all you really need is a set of bocce balls and a place to play. Youth and physical attributes are not essential, and games lasting 20 minutes to an hour are played indoors and out. The length of games depends on the skill of the competitors and the type of game being played (contests governed by international rules tend to be a tad longer).

Bocce players come in all ages and both sexes. Increasingly, the physically and mentally challenged are taking part in the game. Finally, there are very few injuries associated with bocce (okay, so you might drop a ball on your toe occasionally). Sometimes a bocce ball or pallino becomes a dangerous projectile made airborne by a volo or raffa shot. Fences around spectator areas are common and are being constructed with fine mesh to contain the pallino (especially near the ends where the greatest number of balls become missiles). It is safest to watch a game from the sides or from the end of the shooter, rather than from the end toward which the balls are rolling.

Many courts are currently located in social clubs requiring paid membership, but a movement is on to bring the game out of the private sector and into the public. Courts are springing up in public parks. In addition, indoor bocce venues that host parties and corporate outings are opening around the country. Usually outfitted with fine restaurants, these places also offer league play and rent courts by the hour to drop-ins. Campo di Bocce of Livermore and Los Gatos (California), Palazzo di Bocce (Michigan), and Pinstripes (Illinois) are already off and running.

Campo di Bocce of
Livermore, California

Campo di Bocce of Livermore
has outdoor and indoor
courts with fast playing
synthetic surfaces.

Recreational Bocce

Just as Italians brought different dialects to this country – so did they bring regionalized variations of the rules of bocce. A movement toward standardization is gaining momentum, but there is as yet little consistency in the rules of play from one area of the country to another. In Chapter 2 we introduced the game and what have been called Open Rules, a recreational style of play with few regulations. The game can proceed unencumbered by endless restrictions for almost anything goes (more on rules in Chapter 10, Tournament Play & USBF Open Rules).

As we have stated, the game can be played almost anywhere on a variety of surfaces; the backyard, a dirt road, the beach, a golf course, fair grounds or public park. Played on a reasonably level or somewhat hilly surface, the game calls for a variety of skills and strategies and produces rich variations. No two games are ever exactly alike.

The Bocce Shots – Punto, Raffa, and Volo

The playing surface and the position of previously played balls determine which type of delivery is called for. Balls may be rolled gently for point (the punto shot), rolled fast to knock another ball away (the raffa), or lofted in the air (volo). For all bocce shots, the ball must be released before the player oversteps the foul line.

The Punto Shot – Pointing

On smooth, fast surfaces, players tend to roll the ball for point, holding it with palm up or palm down. Players with very good touch like to release smoothly, palm up, letting the ball roll off the fingertips. Executed properly, this imparts a 12 o'clock to 6 o'clock rotation on the ball. This release is much like that of a pure shooter in basketball. The hooper follows through with arm extended high, rolling the ball off the fingertips, and sends the ball sailing toward the basket with good backspin.

A good way to practice this fingertip-release bocce delivery is adapted from an old baseball camp throwing drill. Most young ballplayers' throws miss their targets because of poor grip and/or throwing technique. We place a piece of electrical tape around a baseball and have the player place his middle finger on the stripe and his next fingers to the left and right, with the thumb catching the stripe at the bottom. The baby finger is on the side of the ball. Next, the players enjoy a game of catch, and carefully watch the flight of the ball. With proper grip and throwing motion, the stripe will not wobble as the ball sails to its target.

Wrap a single piece of electrical tape around the center of a bocce ball, grasp it palm up, with the tape running north to south. Use the grip described above (place the middle finger on the tape and one finger on each side of the tape). Since you are rolling with an underhand delivery and the ball is larger, the thumb ends up nearer the top of the ball and not reaching the tape. The little finger rests on the side of the ball for balance, and the roll is executed smoothly off the fingers. Pay close attention to the tape as the ball moves along its path. Thrown properly, the ball reveals a solid black stripe, top to bottom. Any deviation in the stripe or wobbling motion indicates a faulty release (ball coming off the side of the fingers or not coming off fingers evenly).

Many good players roll for point in an entirely different manner. They grip the ball lightly (palm up or down) and toss it a few feet in front of the foul line, releasing all five fingers at once. For them, the touch is in the back swing and release. In either case a good deal of practice is needed to develop the deft release necessary for this most crucial shot in bocce. As we have seen, the game involves strategy, skill and finesse. But, above all, bocce is a game of touch.

Pointing styles differ from player to player.

Note that international rules and USBF Open rules allow you to step on, but not completely over the foul line.

Some Pointers on Pointing

The grip should be light with the palm facing the target. An alternate style is to face the back of the hand to the target. This release helps slow the ball down on fast courts due to backspin, but makes rolling the ball off the fingertips impossible. Proponents of the palm-down toss maintain that it keeps the ball on line better because the backspin tends to "dig in," preventing the ball from diverting left or right. They also feel that there is less chance for the wrist or hand to twist inadvertently during the delivery since this is a more natural position. If you let your hands hang down by your side, you will see that the palm-up release requires an almost 180-degree rotation of the forearm. Try both types of delivery. See what works best for you. The arm should be kept close to the body during the back swing. The right-hander generally places the left foot forward and the lefty has the right foot forward, but this is not a hard and fast rule. Regardless, most of the body weight should be on the front foot, with the back foot on the ground for balance.

Some players place one foot beside the other, and simply bend at the waist and roll. Still others start with both feet together, then deliver while taking a step forward with one foot. Of course, this makes it necessary for the player to begin a step behind the foul line, while the previous methods allow you to cozy right up to it. Some players move forward over the foul line after the ball is released, maintaining that moving directly toward the target promotes better accuracy. Indeed, in recreational play it is not uncommon to see an enthusiastic player toss his ball and run up behind and then alongside it, encouraging and coaxing it toward its destination.

It is important to bend at the waist and keep the body square to the target. Maintain balance and keep the ball and hand at about the same level as the ankle. Keep the arm path straight throughout the delivery, and make a smooth follow-through. The amount of back swing is directly proportional to the distance the ball must travel.

You may sight directly on the target or pick a spot out in front of the release point as some tenpin bowlers do. "Spot bowlers" claim that it is much easier to hit a closer target. Selecting a target zone or drop zone instead of zeroing in on the object ball is a technique that is controversial among bocce players. Some swear by it. Others swear at it. The first group points out that golfers look at the ball, not the hole when putting and that top notch bowlers key on spots on the lane, not the pins. The other group says it's tough to hit what you're not looking at. Give both styles a go, and decide for yourself. Keeping the head down and focusing on the target (target ball or drop zone), even after releasing the ball, helps fosters good concentration. Experiment with all the deliveries and discover what works best for you. Be advised that many of the top players in the world use the drop zone technique.

Ken Dothee, former president of the United States Bocce Federation, reminds us that the arm and hand are on the side of the body, while the eyes are in the center. "Line up your arm with the target, not the center of your body," says Dothee. "This allows you to make a straight release and prevents the arm from crossing in front of your body during the delivery."

Suggestions for Practicing Pointing

To improve accuracy, here is a technique long used by those learning to become fast-pitch softball pitchers. The would-be pitchers first learn the proper grip and delivery, then find a wall to toss against. Initially, they just try to hit the wall anywhere, and field the carom. With success, they move to increasingly smaller targets, trying to hit inside a large chalked box, then a smaller box, and finally a square approximating the size of the strike zone. Bocce's version of this technique involves marking a large circle on your playing surface. Now roll bocce balls with the right amount of force to get them to stop within the ring. As you gain proficiency, make the circle increasingly smaller. If you roll eight balls, it is not enough to land two or three dead center and scatter the rest outside the circle. To develop consistency is to cluster a majority of the balls somewhere in the target zone every time. When you get to this point, shrink the target. It is important to spend enough time developing a high percentage of accuracy with large circles before progressing to smaller ones. Also, decrease the size of the circle by small increments rather than going directly from a large target zone to a small one.

To hone the ability to roll the ball the proper distance, mark two parallel lines across the court and practice rolling balls that come to rest anywhere within these lines. Vary the position of the parallel lines and practice, practice, practice. This drill and the previous one are more enjoyable if practiced with a partner, adding an element of competition to the activity.

To work on controlling the direction or glide path of the bocce ball, create one-foot wide lanes down the court using cones or other marking devices. Roll the ball evenly at different speeds and practice this very important phase of the game. On a level surface, your goal is to roll each ball from one end to the other without dislodging any cones.

To Step or Not to Step When Pointing

We've discussed different styles of release (I prefer the 12 o'clock to 6 o'clock rotation as the ball rolls off the fingertips). I relate it to basketball. The roundball rolls off the fingertips of the best shooters. It sails to the hoop with a pronounced backspin. If you shoot hoops with a kind of knuckleball release, you can learn to be a pretty good shooter. But you'll never become a truly great shooter. It's the fingertip roll that creates the feathery smooth touch of basketball's "pure shooters."

The next technique to address is whether to step forward as you release, or to plant the feet and move only the arm. I've seen excellent pointers utilizing both styles. The following is from the point of view of a right-hander (lefties just reverse things).

Many of the top players cozy right up to the foul line and place their left foot near the chalk mark. Their right foot is well back toward the backboard for balance. The only motion then, comes from the arm. The arm swings back and forth like a pendulum, and the release is on the forward pass. They like the fact that there is no extraneous body motion. Top players, it seems, reach out and roll the ball well out in front of the body.

The alternate release involves taking what has been called a "glide step." A right-hander would take his position a step behind the foul line with feet together. S/he would step with the left foot and release the ball all in one smooth motion. This, proponents say, gets the entire body involved, rather than just the arm, wrist, and hand. Keep the following four S's in mind. The delivery must be Slow, Smooth, and Steady, with the step Straight toward the target.

It is interesting to note that even high level players have quite varied pointing styles. Some step forward as they roll, some plant their feet. Some deliver from directly in front of the body, while others release slightly to the side.

"There is only one rule in pointing" declares journeyman bocce star Dr. Angel Cordano. "Leave the ball in front of the pallino."

The Raffa

The raffa is a fast rolling shot intended to knock an opponent's ball away or to direct the pallino to a new position. For example, your opponent has pallino advantage and rolls the first ball one inch from the object ball. It's probably going to be easier for you to hit that ball away than to roll one closer than an inch from pallino. Some bocce enthusiasts fear that the raffa's increasing popularity will discourage coed play since women's leagues tend to emphasize finesse and strategy over brute strength, but increasingly women players are employing the various hitting techniques. Donna Allen of the USBF maintains that "The key to the successful raffa shot is the follow-through. Therefore, it has been embraced by women over the more physically demanding volo shot." The result is that women, according to Allen, "are becoming more well-rounded and competitive players."

Reminiscent of a break shot in billiards, the raffa is usually made with an approach similar to that of a tenpin bowler. Remember, on all shots the player must release the ball before overstepping the foul line or a foot foul results. Some sets of rules mandate one foul line for pointing and a second for raffa attempts. This second line, farther up the court, allows the bocce player room for several approach steps. Many players intentionally go over the foul line after releasing the ball. Rather than stopping abruptly at the foul stripe, they prefer to improve accuracy by keeping their body's momentum moving in the direction of the target. Other players take a three- or four-step delivery like in bowling, but stop at the foul line. Still others are standing hitters. They stand still, swinging only the arm, hand, and ball to unload a direct hit on the target. Be aware that on some courts the foul lines are painted on the sideboards while on others they are drawn across the surface of the court. In most informal bocce, many players overstep the foul line before releasing the ball and, though this provokes a good deal of grumbling from opponents, foot fouls are rarely called.

The Raffa Technique

As in bowling, players can set their own style of stance, approach and delivery. Rolling a bocce or bowling ball presents fewer absolutes than hitting a baseball or serving a tennis ball. The key is to stay relaxed and comfortable. Some players begin by holding the ball at eye level and sighting over it. Others bend deeply at the waist, and still others hold the ball out at arm's length pointing toward the target. The important thing is to use the exact same stance, approach and delivery every time. You must develop consistency in front of the foul line before you'll see consistent results down by the object ball.

Your initial distance from the foul line depends on the number and size of the steps in your approach (usually three or four). The feet are together or one is slightly ahead of the other. Keep the body square to the foul line and practice until your steps are the same length each time. The steps should be straight (watch out for drifting left or right), slow and under control. The raffa attempt on a bocce court requires the same approach as a strike or spare attempt on the bowling alley, without the slide. If you use a three- or four-step (or five-step) approach at the bowling alley, use the same technique during raffa attempts.

In the three-step approach, the ball drops down and back for the back swing during the first step, which the right-hander takes with the left foot. On the second step the ball is almost at the top of the back swing. The third step is the slide in bowling, with shoulders square to the target and the other arm out for balance. Instead of the slide, the bocce player either stops abruptly upon release, or continues across the foul line *after the release*. The four-step approach is similar to the three-step approach with the additional step beginning with the right foot (for right-handers). Many players need this extra step to bring the entire stance, approach and delivery into synch. Regardless of the number of steps, they must be natural, rhythmic and well-coordinated.

Speed Versus Accuracy

There are many hard hitters in bocce, often an example of overkill. A direct hit with high velocity sends the target ball flying, but often results in a long post-impact roll for the raffa. You've displaced the opponent's close point, but your ball isn't very near to the pallino either. Of course, if you had a previously played ball(s) close to the pallino, a clean takeout of the opponent's ball brings it (them) into scoring position. If you are determined to become a hard thrower, make sure that you do not sacrifice accuracy for speed. Very skilled players impart backspin on their raffa take-out shots, hitting the target solidly and often leaving their ball in almost the same spot as the ball they struck.

Key Points to Emphasize for the Raffa

1. Bend at the waist during the approach and delivery.
2. Keep the arm swing close to the body.

3. The back swing should not be higher than shoulder level.
4. Make the approach steps in a straight line to the target.
5. The first step should be taken by the foot opposite to the throwing arm.
6. Keep the shoulders square to the target.
7. Release the ball on the last step with knees and toes pointing straight at the target.
8. Do not release too soon. Bend at the waist and extend the arm, letting go of the ball out in front of the body (but toward the side of the throwing hand eye).
9. If you prefer rolling off the fingertips, roll the ball like a bowler trying for a strike. If you prefer the loft or lob, then the farther the target the higher your release point should be. Proponents of this method claim that the farther the ball rolls, the more its chance of going off line.
10. Follow through high with a full sweep of the arm.
11. Stress accuracy over speed.
12. Keep the arm path in a straight pendulum-type swing – the arm goes down, back, forward, and to follow-through position in the same constant arc.
13. Make the elements of the stance, approach, delivery and follow-through consistent every time.
14. Emphasize concentration, which is a critical factor in increasing the percentage of hits.

Some Suggestions for Practicing the Raffa

Spend some time working on stance, approach and delivery with no ball. Start by assuming a comfortable starting point and stance, and walk up to the foul line concentrating on just the steps (no arm movement). Next, walk the approach and add the arm swing, delivering an imaginary ball. Now pick up the ball and go through the motion again, but do not roll the ball. Let the weight of the ball do the work of the arm swing. Finally, make a complete approach and delivery rolling at a target. Place target balls at close range for practice until you can hit 80% or better. Then move the target farther away. Remember to make the approach to the launch point slow and smooth and at a constant speed. Fouling often occurs when steps are too long or too fast. Have someone watch you for foot fouls or set up a video camera perpendicular to the foul line. If you have difficulty hitting your target even at close range, try making the target larger by placing several balls in a cluster. As your percentage of hits increases, make the target increasingly smaller, then increasingly farther away. Practice, practice, practice.

Most of the recreational players I meet and play with have the same "flaw" in their game. They can point pretty well, but are weak at hitting. I hear a lot of "Well, I'm not very good at that, so I'll try to close in instead." To be a complete player you must be adept at all facets of the game. Major league baseball teams look for the "multi-tooled player" - the one who can throw, run, field, hit for average, and hit for power. Top flight bocce calls for the deft touch of pointing, the skillful precision of hitting, and the proper use of tactics to know when to do which.

The first step for recreational players is to go ahead and try to hit when the situation warrants it. You won't get any better at hitting by avoiding it. Consider this...a very shrewd basketball coach once told me that, "A good shooter is a bad shooter who kept shooting." Keep hitting.

Start practicing by putting your target fairly close and don't move it back until you can consistently hit it at that short range. You decide what consistency level is right for you (70%, 80%, more, less?). If your goal is 90% hitting accuracy, don't move the target back until you can hit it 9 times out of 10. Good basketball free throw shooters sometimes end practice by making ten foul shots in a row. You might think that ten straight is not so many for a skilled player, but the shooter in this drill counts only swishes. Balls that go in, after first hitting the backboard, rim or flange don't count ("nothing but net" is the goal). Adapt this strategy to your hitting practice so that hits only count if they drive the target toward the backboard. Any glancing blow that sends the target veering to the left or right doesn't count. For even more challenging accuracy, use the pallino for the target rather than a bocce ball. Having a practice partner or two at the other end makes for efficient use of time. They practice hitting back toward your end, conveniently returning the balls for your next set.

Note: In international play, a raffa may not be rolled all the way to its target. There are court lines at points A, B, and C. Your release for a raffa is at point B, but the ball must pass point C before it strikes the ground (see Chapter 11 – International Play).

The Volo

Note: The suggestions listed here apply to the volo shot in backyard or recreational settings. True international volo shots must meet certain additional restrictions. See Chapter 11, International Play. Many open rules tournaments outlaw the volo because of insurance liability, and others disallow the shot on short courts figuring that it is too easy to hit close targets, or because they don't want the court surface pitted with volo induced divots.

When playing on grass, rough, or soft surfaces, it is often necessary to loft the ball into the air, letting it bounce and then run to the target. This is a form of what bocce players call the volo shot (an aerial toss). The volo, traditionally used to knock an opponent's ball away, allows for better accuracy than rolling on rough, uneven surfaces. With practice altering the height and distance of the lob and analyzing the subsequent roll of the ball, a player can add this effective weapon to his arsenal of shots.

Some players loft the ball half way or more toward the target and let it run the rest of the way. The volo shot can be controlled by holding the ball palm down, or palm up. Sometimes you will need to throw it with backspin to get it to stop quickly after it lands. For very long volos, you may want to toss the ball with the palm facing up to impart more forward spin thus increasing its post-landing carry. In any case, unless your lawn is very level, it is often difficult to roll for points on grass with consistent results.

A variation of this shot is good for dealing with a rough surface just in front of the playing line. Simply lob the ball over the rough area and let it roll to the target. For a short lob, release the ball at about the level of the knee. The faster the surface, the higher the release point and trajectory. For high loft shots, the release point should be at the level of the upper thigh or above. The longer the toss, the more exaggerated the back swing must be. Swing the arm in a straight line with the target and push off the legs on the release. Follow through high. Practice by placing an object on the playing surface over which the ball must pass on its way to the target.

The traditional volo shot is tossed into the air in an attempt to strike its target on the fly. A skillful player can make a neat transfer of energy shot in which his ball hits the opponent's ball, sending it flying but leaving his ball in the approximate spot that it struck (often referred to as "changing colors," e.g. the red ball "changed" to green). Another option is to strike the ground with the volo a foot or two before the target, and have it hit the target on the roll. After the initial impact, the volo's energy of motion is transferred to the target ball which ricochets away leaving your ball in contention. However, depending on the type of surface and the kind of ball used, a short volo can bounce right over its target.

For both the raffa and the volo there is a very
athletic approach before release of the ball.

Top bocce players use an approach similar to the raffa approach when delivering a volo. However, the stance and approach are much more upright and the ball is usually tossed with palm down (although I am seeing more and more palm up style volo shots). Most volo shooters use a four-step approach and continue moving past the foul line directly toward the target after they release the ball. We suggest mastering the stationary throw before progressing to this technique.

The Volo Technique

Begin working on the last two steps of the four-step approach since these are the most critical. During these steps the arm swing and launch is made. Breaking down and mastering these two steps, then, is essential before advancing.

Stand at the foul line with feet together and arms by the side. Take two steps backward to bring yourself into correct position for this drill. The first step is taken with the foot opposite the throwing arm. As this step is taken, bring the arm swing back in a straight pendulum-like movement. The arm should be at the top of the back swing as the second step is started. The arm comes forward to the launch point on the second step. Continue to move forward toward the target after you release the ball. This follow-through fosters better accuracy, and is not a foot foul unless you overstep the line before releasing the shot.

Once the two-step approach is mastered, advance to the four-step method. Begin four steps from the foul line with feet together and arms by the side. Many players prefer a stance with the ball held at waist, chest or eye level. With this stance the ball is often held palm up and rotated into palm down position during the arm swing. Again, the first step should be with the foot opposite to the throwing hand. The arm does not begin the back swing on this step. The back swing begins on the second step and should not reach the top of its arc until the end of the third step. The fourth step brings the arm forward in a straight line with the target and the ball is released. During the follow-through phase, the player continues moving in a straight line to the target, promoting greater accuracy. Use the same suggestions for practicing raffa shots listed previously for honing your volo skills. Using two sets of bocce balls when working on the volo and raffa shots makes for a more efficient practice session (more repetitions before walking to the other end of the play area to "reload"). Another option is to practice with a partner stationed at the other end. You shoot at targets at his end and he returns the balls to your end with his practice shots.

Compete at Your Own Level

With bocce's flexibility and simplicity there is a style and level of play for you. But we must warn you - the game grows on you and eventually you may yearn to play at the next higher level. You start out playing on the backyard lawn and long for a court. You play on the court and you want to join a league or participate in tournaments. It is inevitable. Don't fight it. The beauty of the game is that it can be enjoyed on so many different levels – from recreational play in your backyard on grass, dirt, or gravel to more structured play at the social club or outdoor courts. For some, tournament play involving singles, doubles, triples, or four-person teams is the way to go. And tournament play ranges from the very low key to the extremely cutthroat (see Chapter 10, Tournament Play & USBF Open Rules). Bocce players can even compete at the national and international level, representing their country in world championship tournaments. And the International Olympics Committee has recognized bocce as a sport. This is an important first step toward it becoming an Olympic sport.

Bocce is about to explode in this country. LL Bean's summer catalog advertises bocce balls in a handsome carrying case and, yes, designer bocce shoes are in vogue. "Bocce," said one thirty-something couple, "is the yuppiest thing we do." Bocce's small but enthusiastic band of promoters expects it to become one of the top recreational sports in the USA. A set of bocce balls will be as common a household item as a television set. Experiencing ever-rising popularity, indoor bocce courts are sprouting up in restaurants, lounges and sports bars in various parts of the country. You can play some friendly bocce while waiting to be served, or play a game to settle the bill.

The introduction of bocce in American schools is beginning to gain momentum, with young people taking to the game readily. In Wilbraham, Massachusetts, bocce buff Leonard Hickey built a gorgeous 76-foot long court on his business property. He installed spectator benches, and lights the court from dusk to dawn. Local high school students spend some evenings there and are proving to be bocce naturals. They understand the game immediately and are rapidly developing their own bocce jargon.

"You scored the point, so you get pallino privilege – it's like having the honors in golf."

"That ball is too close to beat, so take it out!"

"Yea, it's near the sideboard, so run the rail!"

"Good idea, even if you miss, we have three pellets left."

Maria Colangelo, a teacher of Italian at Plainville High in Connecticut runs a bocce week that culminates with a popular bocce tournament. The tourney is open only to students in her classes, a strategy that has boosted course enrollment over the years. The students practice bocce on the lawns on campus, then play at a local Italian club where the members serve as referees. The players are permitted to speak only Italian when asking questions of the referee, and of course, the official can only respond via the romance language. Ms. Colangelo's excellent program is well covered by local media, and is typical of the response bocce will get in schools in the future.

It is amazing that within such a simple and elegant framework of play, bocce provides such limitless variation. From backyard lawns to international competitions, bocce is truly a game for all people. And in what other arena could an 80-year-old grandparent compete with an eight-year-old grandchild and be on nearly equal terms?

Play at the Nevins Memorial Library (Methuen, MA) Youth Bocce Tourney. According to the library's children's director, the annual event is the most eagerly anticipated program of the summer.

The popular tourney, held on the grounds of the
library, often evokes great excitement, the thrill of
victory, and sometimes the agony of defeat.

Eagle-Tribune photographer Katie McMahon caught this
young woman experiencing the Joy of Bocce and won
a "top photo of the year" award in the process.

CHAPTER 5

THE GAME AS PLAYED ON COURTS

While lawn bocce is very exciting and serves the sporting needs of a great many people, some feel a need to advance to the next level. Playing bocce on a court with stone dust, clay or artificial surface brings the game to that higher plane. Bocce games played on courts generally take place in social clubs or in public parks. The play may be informal "pickup" games or structured as leagues. For league games between two social clubs, three games to a match is common, after which the hosts generally provide drinks and/or dinner. Increasingly, especially in areas that have no public courts, bocce lovers are building their own backyard courts (instructions in Chapter 8).

"Official" courts are 60, 70, 80 feet and longer in different areas of the country. The court game is quite different from playing in an open park where whoever has the pallino can choose the direction to roll it. In many ways the court version of bocce is similar to the game played on lawns, but it magnifies the importance of strategy and planning moves ahead.

When my family and I play lawn bocce there's no telling where the pallino will end up. Sometimes even clever strategy goes for naught. But, on our backyard court, I know the object ball will stay somewhere within the wooden banks of the 10 x 76 foot alley. I can plan what to do with each ball accordingly. Also, playing on courts includes a new dimension of skillfully played bank shots.

Finesse is a bigger factor on courts due to the fast surface of a fine, hard packed stone dust, clay or oyster shell top dressing. The ball cruises along on a seemingly frictionless path. Since it travels such a distance with little energy supplied by the player, finesse and touch are critical. Players need to develop a smooth release of the ball and soft touch to achieve success. In addition, the raffa and volo shots can be perfected on courts because the lumps, bumps and other surface abnormalities of the lawn are eliminated.

Even when played on official courts, bocce is not a physically demanding sport. Some claim physical benefits, like walking back and forth to play both ends and bending/lifting to pick up the balls. You're using the large muscle groups of the upper and lower body, but an aerobic workout it's not. There is no pounding on your spine and knees as in basketball, no sprinting and sliding as in baseball, and no oxygen deprivation as in tennis or racquetball. You don't have to be in shape to play bocce, though physical fitness controls the fatigue factor in any competitive sport. On the other hand, the mental and social benefits of bocce are incalculable. Competing on courts or grass fosters a healthy outlook on life. And after all, bocce meets today's health and fitness standard of favoring lifetime sports over those that you can enjoy only in your youth.

Elite players maintain that fitness is a major factor in large, double elimination tournaments. Some have competed almost around the clock, from 9:00 a.m. to midnight and beyond. Furthermore, they claim that the rapid-fire shoot-out competitions held at major bocce events are among the most physically demanding endeavors in sports. Reminiscent of the NBA's three-point shoot-out, bocce's rapid-fire drill gives players the opportunity to show off their volo-ing ability. Competitors run from one end of the court to the other attempting to score as many hits as possible within a five-minute time limit. As you can imagine, five minutes of continuous running and tossing bocce balls in the air can make for a very tiring exercise. See Chapter 11 – International Play for more on the volo shoot-out. Take a good look at the international game (punto raffa volo). You might like it. It is a pretty athletic game, the antithesis of the stereotypical "old man's game" of bocce. Young athletic types are gravitating to it.

Initial Toss of the Pallino

The game is more structured on the court; its rules more clearly refined, if not uniform. First off, there are rules governing the initial toss of the pallino. Again, there is no standardization of the rules, it being played differently from one area to another even within the same country. See Chapter 10 for USBF Open Rules, which many hope will become the standard.

Most rules specify that the pallino must travel a minimum distance – usually beyond the half-court marker and a minimum distance from the end board. Besides the required distance that the pallino must reach, some rules stipulate that it must come to rest a minimum distance from the side walls. The now defunct International Bocce Association, formerly of Utica, New York, developed a set of rules that are still widely used in the East. They require the first toss of the pallino reach mid-court or beyond, and settle at least four feet from the end board and 12 inches from the sideboard. If the initial toss of the pallino does not satisfy all of these requirements, the pallino is returned to the player for another attempt. IBA rules give the player three attempts to successfully place the pallino, after which it goes to the other team for one attempt. If that try fails, the referee places the pallino in a legal position and play resumes. The team with pallino advantage (the one who made the three unsuccessful attempts) still tosses the first ball. See USBF Open Rules - Chapter 10 for a more modern approach to the initial toss of the pallino.

Note: In recreational play, when the pallino fails to settle within legal parameters, players often agree to speed up the game by simply moving it to a legal position. For example, if the ball comes to rest eight inches from the left sideboard, they move it four inches or so to the right. If it settles three feet from the end board, they bring it forward a foot.

Foul Lines

Official courts have foul lines that players may not step over until they release the ball. Some rules stipulate a single foul line (at each end of the court), others mandate two foul lines – one for pointing and one for hitting. The reasoning for the second foul line is that many players use a three- or four-step approach when hitting (called spocking in some areas). The pointing line does not allow enough runway for this shot, so a second hitting line, closer to the target, is used. In any case, the player must release the ball before passing the foul line. The first foot foul committed by each player sometimes results in a warning, and subsequent fouls carry penalties. Both raffa and volo players can use the hitting line as their release point. Standing hitters may position themselves right at the hitting line when attempting a raffa or volo.

Note: International rules mandate one line for pointing and raffa hitting, and a second for volo hitting (often, a volo approach involves even more steps than a raffa).

Pre-Game Warm-Ups

In tournaments and some recreational play, the participants roll a frame in each direction to get acclimated to the court. During this once-up and once-back practice, players attempt the various shots (punto, raffa, volo) and look for irregularities and tendencies in the surface before actual play begins. Pay close attention to how the ball rolls at various speeds. Look for any clues that might help you play various shots during the ensuing game. Play a ball or two off the sideboard to see if the carom is as you expect. Toss a raffa off the backboard to check how much bounce back you get.

Playing the Game

Regardless of the surface on which you play bocce, the roll for point is the game's most important skill. You may be able to "get by" without a raffa or volo shot, but if you cannot point, you cannot compete well in bocce. A complete player needs to be able to point *and* hit, but, just as the fastball is the king of pitches in baseball, the punto is sovereign in the kingdom of bocce.

When an opponent's point is too close to outlag, good players use the raffa or volo to try to knock it away. The ideal knock-away ball strikes its target, sends it out of contention, and then settles in for the point. Even if the hit is good but the opponent's ball is still in, at least there should be room to close in for the score on the next roll. If the shot misses its mark, however, the shooter must decide if it is worth the risk to try another knock-away shot. The percentages may be better for closing in to keep the opponent from scoring multiple points.

Some good players try to hit away a ball even though it is not extremely close. They want to have one of their team's balls at the backboard in case the opponents knock the object ball there later in the game. They reason that a good hit eliminates the opponent's point, and a miss puts a ball at the backboard acting as a kind of insurance policy. (Note: this won't work in USBF Open Rules because any ball that hits the backboard without first touching another ball is removed from play for the remainder of the frame.) Purists say that there is too much play off the side and backboards, especially when the backboard is played "live". In some areas of the country, players look for every opportunity to take the object ball to the backboard. Then they simply pound the end board to score points. Purists don't want the game dominated by play in the end zone; they want it played in the open court where luck is less a factor and touch is the dominating skill. "These guys think the game is billiards," commented one disgruntled bocce enthusiast unhappily watching balls carom off the back and sideboards. "Some of them even make the first toss of pallino off the side board," he added. "What game are they playing?"

Think things over...then execute.
Photos by Jack O'Heir

Consider the following common scenario: Team A tosses the pallino and brings its first ball several inches away from it. Team B tries an unsuccessful raffa and elects to try a second knock-away shot. That one misses too, leaving two of Team B's balls at the end board. Team B, after some thought, attempts a third raffa, this time driving the pallino to the backboard. The raffa shot rolls to the end board, too. Now, three of Team B's balls are IN, even though only one of their shots was a hit. Scenarios like this are spurring a movement to institute the rule stating that a ball that hits the backboard without first hitting a ball on the court is "burned" or declared "dead". The dead ball is removed from the court, and may not score a point. Again, purists want the rules to favor the player with skill and touch. Some bocce enthusiasts want to go as far as marking the position of the balls (like they do in international play) when the object ball is near the backboard or whenever a missed volo or raffa is likely. The player must then call his shot, and if he misses and displaces other balls, all balls may be returned to their original positions (bocce's *rule of advantage* would apply, in which case the opponents could elect to return the scattered balls to their original positions, or leave them in their new locations).

Most courts have a swing board or bumper board (see Chapter 8, Building a Backyard Court) at each end that serves to absorb the force of a ball's impact. Again, this design is to keep players from using the backboard as a rebounding instrument, first rifling a raffa off the board, then watching it carom back toward the pallino. The idea is to entice players to score points by using the more skillful, smooth roll.

Shot Selection

Before each shot, stand at the backboard and analyze the situation. Select which type of shot is appropriate for the current lay of the balls. Make a quick mental picture of the distance and layout of the previously played balls. Pause briefly to let the picture come into focus. Now form a mental image of the successful completion of the shot you will attempt. Finally, block everything else out of your mind – the score, the fans, the opponents – and execute.

The smooth roll for point is the most common shot in bocce. Most players use it and one of the two knock-away shots (raffa or volo) in their game. Currently, there are very few bocce players using the volo technique here on the East Coast. You should try to master both the raffa and volo techniques. Both are a bit awkward at first, but with practice they can become successful parts of your game. When I was first introduced to the correct raffa and volo styles, I resisted. I wasn't comfortable. "Why use a bowling-type run-up approach?" I thought. "You can't slide on a bocce court." And overstepping the foul line after releasing the ball didn't sit well with me either. But, after I built my own backyard court and practiced proper technique, the shots became more natural and welcome additions to my game.

Thinking Ahead

Before choosing the type of shot to attempt, think about the consequences of the shot. If I roll a ball here, what will my opponent likely do? Do I want to stay short of the target so as not to nudge the pallino toward an opponent's ball? Or do I want to be long so that I might push the pallino toward my own team's previously played ball(s). When I introduced my friend, Walter Pare, to bocce, he called the game "lawn chess". "You can think ahead and know the move you want to make" says Pare, "but you can't always place the pieces exactly where you want them."

Playing Bank Shots

One of the neat things about playing on a court is the opportunity to deftly execute bank shots. I tend to agree with the purists who want the game in the open court, away from the side and end boards. Nevertheless, a well-placed shot that caroms off the sideboard and slips in between two other balls and steals the point is one of the nicest feelings that bocce has to offer. (Note that international rules prohibit play off the side and end boards.) Bank shots are mastered by experimenting. Practice hitting the boards at different angles and at different speeds. Watch the caroms and make mental notes of the results.

Moving the Pallino to Gain Advantage

Be aware that the position of the pallino may change at any time during a frame. A well-placed raffa or volo attempt can save the day by redirecting the pallino away from one team's balls and toward the other's. Consider where your opponent may try to move the pallino to gain an advantage, and how you can minimize the chance of this happening. Often, this simply means keeping a ball near the end board to prevent the other team from scoring easy points by bringing the object ball there. Or it can mean intentionally leaving a ball short, and in front of the pallino, blocking the path of your opponents' subsequent attempts.

Courting Bocce

Bocce may be the sleeping giant of sports. For it to really explode in America, many more courts need to be constructed. The sport needs more visibility, more exposure. Promoters are looking for media coverage and corporate support for big time tournament action. They are also trying to introduce bocce into school systems, but, while permanent courts are being installed in schools around the country, this is being greeted with mixed results. This is reminiscent of the introduction of soccer into American schools. Officials were skeptical at first, but soccer flourishes today because people realized how inexpensive and easy it was to initiate soccer programs. The same is true for bocce.

According to demographic research done by the United States Bocce Federation, the average age of the American bocce player has decreased by almost 20 years since the 1980's (when it was age 60). The visibility of the game has increased dramatically due to the construction of outdoor facilities. Bocce is especially popular in states like California and Florida where residents play outdoors year round. Some employers are even building courts on job sites, creating a pleasant diversion for hardworking people. Installing signs that summarize the rules and give a little history of the game serves to prevent vandalism and misuse of the courts (in one California park, visitors used the bocce courts as horseshoe pits). Bocce promoters hope to get bocce courts in schools, park and recreation departments, senior centers, youth clubs, new housing developments, hospitals, and even correctional facilities. While seeking corporate and business sponsorships, the ultimate goal is to increase tournament exposure and lure the television market.

For the sport to continue its growth, it must have standardization of equipment and courts. Today bowling balls, pins, and alleys are uniform across the country. There is no reason the same consistency can't be true of bocce.

Bocce Etiquette

1. Don't take too long thinking over a shot.
2. Don't over-coach or tell teammates what to do on each shot. Make suggestions. But, to execute well, a player needs to feel comfortable with the shot that he'll attempt.
3. Don't wander off – stay with the team even when you have completed delivery of your allotted bocce balls.
4. Be ready to play when it's your turn.
5. Stay under emotional control at all times.
6. Remain quiet while others take their turn.
7. After each frame, leave balls in place until the referee officially awards points.
8. Losing team buys the drinks.

Variations of Play

In 1995 the Special Olympics World Games were held in Connecticut, and I served as one of the bocce referees. During the rare "down time" when we weren't officiating, we played bocce with some of the Connecticut locals. They insisted that the initial toss of the "pill" had to come to rest at least 12 inches from the side boards. If it stopped say, eight inches or so from the side, one player would give it a gentle kick into legal position (approximately 12 inches from the board) rather than roll it back to the player to try again. This kept the game moving, they reasoned. The position of the object ball (now in the same general area as the person rolling it intended) is not going to unfairly favor one team or the other.

At the North Carolina SO World Games in 1999 we encountered locals who played a fascinating variation. They favored teams of four players, each rolling one ball. Furthermore, the balls are marked 1, 2, 3, and 4 with indelible ink. Teams must decide at the start of the game who will be first roller, second, etc. This order may not be altered during the course of play. This, they claimed, negated an outstanding player's skills. For example, a player couldn't say "Tom, you take this short. You're better at hitting than I am." The sequence can never be altered.

Another difference to their play was in the "hitting". They never rolled with speed to knock an opponent's ball away. They rolled almost as if for point, gently nudging the opponent's ball out of position and leaving their ball close to the target. Conventional wisdom is that faster speeds make for truer rolls, but it was hard to argue with the uncanny accuracy we witnessed in North Carolina.

Forty-five Degree Angle Boards

More than a couple of "old timers" have told me about playing bocce with 45 degree angle boards at each end. You could carom your shot off these to direct your ball into scoring position.

Tom Coyle uses these 45 degree angle boards - a style of play that he picked up in Phillipsburg, New Jersey.

"I placed the corner boards, thinking all courts had them. I later found out that nobody else has them and am now considering their removal if I want better players to arrange home-and-home matches with me. But the people who play on my court absolutely love them."

To stop players from always playing off the angle and end boards, Tom made a rule that "any ball thrown to backboard without first hitting a sideboard or another ball is removed from play for that inning."

The angle boards make it "a little easier to keep the lower skilled teams in the game" and his rules discourage ricocheting balls off the back and favor pointing or "coodling in" as he calls it.

Bob Goetz of North Carolina says he's seen the 45 degree angle courts in Cleveland, Ohio. "It makes for a fun and interesting game. For example, one can ride the ball down the far right corner, and with sufficient speed, catch the left hand corner (basically reversing the direction from the start of the throw) and back to the pallino. This is a very effective shot, especially when the pallino seems surrounded heavily in front by other balls."

Mercy/Slaughter/Skunk Rule

Stan Stanton of Las Vegas coined the phrase "kill the skunk" when trying to eliminate a shut-out shortened game – thus preventing getting "skunked." "Colorful language for a wonderful game" he mused.

A "skunk rule" is not common in bocce but in some parts of New Hampshire, 8-0 invokes a "mercy rule" or "slaughter rule".

"If you are behind that far, you're probably overmatched, so let's get the next game going" is one perspective. And "Behind 8-0 means you are behind. It doesn't mean you've lost" is the other.

I'm the type of player that never gives up - a holdover from my days in the dog-eat-dog world of competitive basketball and baseball. There is nothing more exhilarating than coming back from a big deficit and winning. One baseball season, when I was coaching the local high school team, we faced a must-win situation on the final day of the season. A victory would make us conference champs, sending us to the state tourney. A loss would probably relegate us to second place. The other team jumped on us right away with multiple runs in the early innings. In short order we were down 14-1 coming to bat in the sixth inning (high school baseball hereabouts is a seven-inning affair). I got the troops together, put substitutes in the game, and said things like "Let's bat for a half-hour" and "Hey, this is gonna be a comeback story you'll tell your grandchildren about." Then the most incredible thing happened. We batted for 31 minutes, sending 20 batters to the plate. There were 12 hits, and 5 walks, but no errors. We ended up winning the contest and the conference championship. The non-starters that I put in when the game was seemingly out of hand went 8 for 8 - shows what a clever coach I am. Most of the parents had gone home when we fell behind in the late innings, and our players had trouble convincing them that we really did win the game.

We were part of something very special that day - something that a "mercy rule" or "slaughter rule" would have prevented. I'm against shortening games in this manner unless you are running a large tournament and need to keep to a tight schedule.

Backboard Dead

There is a movement afoot (a good one, I think) to make any ball that hits the backboard without first hitting another bocce ball or the pallino a "dead" ball. The ball is removed from the court ("burned") and may not score a point that frame. This is a compromise of sorts between the strict International Rules and today's wide variety of "Open" rules. International rules include "calling" shots, and marking the positions of previously played balls (which are returned to their original positions if the caller fails to make an accurate shot). Even top players think that the international rules are a "tough sell" for most recreational players in this country. Critics claim that international play is too complicated and makes the game long and dull.

The movement though, is toward making the game one of touch and finesse, while minimizing the luck factor. In the East where some play everything "live" off the backboard, they often attempt to hit away an opponent's close point early in a frame. If they miss, they reason, "That's okay. I wanted a ball at the back anyway, in case the opposition knocks the pallino there later." With the backboard always live, a poor shot may become a good shot later.

In some areas they play the back wall dead no matter how a ball got there. Say you try to knock away a close point and miss. If your missed attempt hits the backboard, it is dead (taken out of the court and not figured in the scoring for that end). If your shot successfully hits its target and causes the struck ball to hit the back wall, then that ball is dead. Furthermore, if you hit your target causing it to roll to the back and your ball has sufficient momentum so that it too hits the back, then it also is dead.

I think that somewhere in bocce's past (all of these games - bocce, bowls, boules - have their evolution lost in the mists of antiquity), the game was played with ditches at both ends. Causing an opponent's ball to end up in the ditch was a big advantage - it couldn't score a point.

Part of me likes the idea that you play the home team's rules when you visit their court, and they play your rules when they come to your venue. It's part of the charm and fascination of the game. The variations are testimony to the enduring appeal of an activity that evolved in different parts of the world, is played somewhat differently from place to place, yet whose basic idea is the same. Let's see who can roll, toss or otherwise deliver their bocce balls closest to the object ball.

Yet, another part of me cries out for standardization so that the game can advance to the level of say, professional bowling. Hey, I like bowling, but bocce has it all over bowling. It has a cerebral aspect that I don't see in just knocking down pins. If bowling can achieve such a high level, there is no reason bocce can't as well.

Chapter 6

The Equipment

One of the neat things about bocce is that you need very little equipment to enjoy the game. All that is required is a set of bocce balls that, with proper care, can last a lifetime. Be aware, though, that top players purchase new sets several times a year. Reasoning that a couple of nicks and scratches on a ball's surface could alter its path to the target, they aren't taking any chances. And, at the other end of the competitive spectrum, many recreational, backyard lawn players use an "anything goes" style of play where the object ball is "live" no matter where it ends up (in the woods, ravine, creek, stream, just about anywhere). As you might expect, more than a few pallinos get lost and need to be replaced.

Sure, there are designer shoes and apparel and exotic measuring devices, but these are extras. My family and friends played backyard bocce for years with nothing more than a good set of bocce balls. We didn't even own a fancy measuring device. The points that we couldn't call by eye were measured with our feet, hands, twigs, string, an old car antenna or a standard tape measure. For many of us, though, bocce becomes almost an obsession. We want to read and learn more about it, practice and play more often, and explore bocce related paraphernalia. What follows is a brief primer on the equipment and their distributors. There are some pretty neat gadgets and bocce gear that make terrific gifts for the bocce buff in your life. I've spent a good deal of time and effort evaluating equipment, and you can learn more about many of these at www.joyofbocce.com.

Bocce Balls

First, don't buy an inferior set of bocce balls just to save a few dollars. The balls may be the only bocce-related purchase you'll ever make, so it should be a cost-effective one. A good quality set may include a warranty of up to five years. Bocce balls specifications vary slightly from one manufacturer to another (the international standards are metric - 107 mm and 920 g). Pallinos vary in size too, depending on the manufacturer. The international standard is 40 mm, but many recreational sets come with larger target balls (50 mm and larger). Most dealers package a set of eight balls and a pallino. This usually includes four balls of one color, four of another color, and a pallino of a third color. Bocce balls traditionally were made of wood, but today are of composition material much like bowling balls (some international play mandates metal balls). Some sets further distinguish the four balls of each color with engraved marks to tell one teammate's balls from another. This is of dubious advantage since telling which teammate threw which ball is not nearly as important as telling which team's ball is which.

If you are going to play exclusively on grass, try to avoid the smaller object balls. Small pallinos tend to be obscured even by closely cropped lawns. My family has used a croquet ball or field hockey ball as the object ball when playing on grass, and the bocce pallino when we're on the court. Some manufacturers include a carrying case with the set of balls, others offer it as an extra item. Careful – some of the more expensive European balls come four to a set instead of eight and don't include a pallino (and metal balls are sold in sets of two). Really competitive players cart their personal bocce balls wherever they play. They want the consistency that using the same bocce balls every game brings. You'll often see them use a cloth or chamois to wipe dust and debris from the ball before each toss.

Bocce Ball Dealers

Many U.S. sporting goods manufacturers and dealers offer bocce sets for sale. You will find bocce balls under the names of outfits like Sport-Craft and Eddie Bauer. You can visit the sporting goods departments at places like Target, but be advised that the popularity of bocce in your area will have an impact on the store's inventory. Department store bocce sets may have been made in and imported from China or Taiwan.

Italian-Made Bocce Balls

Super Martel and Perfetta are well regarded Italian-made bocce balls. Visit www.joyofbocce.com for links to sites that retail these high-end, high quality bocce sets.

Perfetta and Super Martel bocce balls have a great reputation for quality and exacting measurement standards. They offer sets for true international competition as well as those for recreational play. "Professional" sets from Perfetta and Super Martel are sold in sets of four (you bring your set and your opponents bring their set).

An excellent choice—Perfetta Bocce Set—Italian-made—high quality—4 red , 4 green, white pallino, carry bag.

International punto raffa volo rules state that bocce balls must be 107 mm in diameter with a weight of 920 grams. The pallino must be 40 mm in diameter and weigh 60 grams. Though you may never play international rules, the 107 mm size should be your first criterion in selecting bocce balls. Unless you have large hands, balls bigger than 107 mm tend to be too large to control easily, especially with volo shooting. Some balls are as large as 115 mm or more.

A Word About the Playing Rules that Accompany Your Purchase

There are many different sets of rules that govern bocce play in America. The only rules that are standardized are the true international rules discussed in Chapter 11. Any set of rules that comes with your purchase should be taken for what it is – a set of rules. Various groups, trying to gain a foothold in the sport, have made deals with manufacturers to insert their version of the rules and court dimensions into each bocce set sold. One mandates a 60- by 12-foot court (short by many other groups' standards). The point is that these are one group's "official" specifications for the game. There are others. Consider our Chapters 8 and 10 before accepting any group's court layout or playing rules as law.

Bocce Carry Bag

If, for some reason, you have a set of bocce balls but need a carry bag, I recommend one of heavy duty nylon material. These are generally 9" X 9" X 9", and hold 8 balls and 1 pallino. Most feature a zipper and perhaps a velcro closure. Some dealers offer metal, plastic or wooden crates, but the nylon bag is the way to go.

Measuring Devices

In informal recreational bocce, you can get by without a formal measuring device, using hands, feet, string, twigs, car antenna, or other household objects to determine points. Most families have a standard tape measure in the garage or workshop, and that works very well, especially for long measurements. We recommend metric measurements over English. When comparing very similar lengths, gauging centimeters is easier than calculating eighths and sixteenths of an inch. Be advised though, that some bocce measures have no calibrations. We don't need to know the actual distance between the balls in contention and the pallino, just which one is closer. The ever-ready tape measure is a staple at most spirited bocce games. Often, the sport produces something akin to a football huddle – a crowd engulfing the object ball anxiously awaiting the results of a measurement.

Measuring Via Geometry

Believe it or not, you can skip the measuring device and use the Pythagorean Theorem to determine which ball is IN. Stand by the bocce balls and form a triangle with the object ball (pallino) at the apex (see photo).

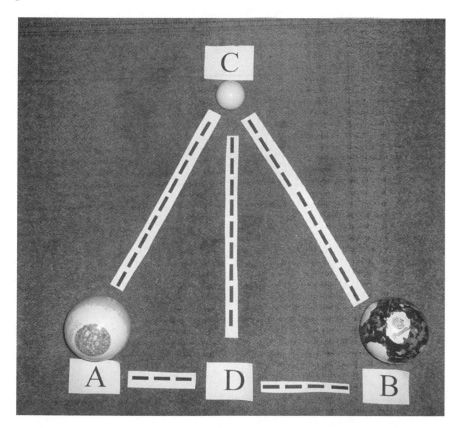

1) Draw an imaginary line (A - B) between the two bocce balls (see photo - RED to the left, GREEN to the right).
2) Now draw an imaginary perpendicular (C - D) from the pallino to line segment AB
3) Since AD is obviously shorter than DB, then AC has to be shorter than BC...so the RED ball is in. If you had known this strategy in high school, I bet you would have tried to stay awake in geometry class. This might also indicate, as previously suspected, that the ancient Greeks played some serious bocce.

People send me many photos of bocce players measuring for points with various tape measures. Usually they are holding one end of the tape at the pallino, then extending the tape over the top center of the ball being measured (or vice-versa). This is okay to get a general idea of which ball is closer, but for accuracy you need *inside measure*. Place the tape measure between the object ball and bocce ball and see how much tape needs to be extended between the two.

There are many measuring devices specifically designed for the ball-and-target games of bocce, boules, and lawn bowls. The following are some that I've tested and recommend. They are available at JoyofBocce.com.

Remember: when measuring for point in bocce, we don't have to know the actual distance in inches or centimeters. We just need to know which ball is closer to the object ball.

Premier Boule Measure

This is a small, slender metric tape measure that extends to two meters (more than six feet). The tape is self-locking when extended, and to retract it you have to press a release button on top. It is best to hold on to the tape as you press the button to ensure that the internal rewind mechanism does not get fouled. There are no calibrations on the steel tape. We aren't measuring the actual distance between the balls, just determining which one is closer.

A thin plastic post extends about a centimeter from the back end of the measure. When measuring, this post is placed against the pallino. To use this device, place it on the ground between the pallino and the ball in question. Place the rear post against the pallino and extend the tape until it touches the bocce ball. The tape will remain extended to this length. Move over to the other bocce ball in contention, and compare measurements.

This measure has calipers for evaluating shorter lengths. The calipers extend from the base of the measure and fold neatly out of the way when not in use. And if all of this is not enough for you, the implement will even keep score. On one side, it has a clever spinning wheel arrangement that tracks two team's scores up to 21.

Clubhawk Gold Bowls Measure

Using a string rather than a steel tape, this is an extremely accurate measuring device (popular with lawn bowls players in England). It extends a couple feet farther than the Premier, has the same calipers for close measurements, and even has a belt clip.

Remember, we don't need a finely calibrated instrument that measures exactly how far a ball is from the object ball...we just need to know which is closer to it. This nifty string device does the trick. You pull out enough string to reach the first ball you are measuring. If you have to pull more string from the housing to reach the other ball in contention...then IT is farther away!

To the right of the bocce balls are the Premier, the
Clubhawk and the Henselite measuring devices.

Henselite Bowls Measure

This is a small metal telescopic device not much bigger than a ball point pen (approximately six inches when closed). It's an ingenious tool for inside measurement. The player or referee first estimates the distance between the pallino and the two bocce balls to be compared. Then, he extends the appropriate telescopic sections to a length slightly less than that estimate. Next, he places the device between the pallino and one of the balls in question and extends it until it touches both balls. The head of the tool is equipped with a screw-top mechanism. Turning the top in one direction lengthens the tool, while winding in the opposite direction shortens it (one mm per 360-degree rotation). This fine-tuning makes for very precise measuring. Finally, the measurer places the device between the pallino and the other ball and compares. Extra care must be taken with this device. A careless person might easily disturb the positions of balls being measured.

Like a ball point pen, the Henselite Bowls Measure has a clasp for fastening onto your shirt pocket. Fully extended, it is one meter (approximately 39 inches) long, so you'll still need a tape for longer measures. For measurements less than the length of the tool, it has calipers that fold out of the way when not needed. These calipers are capable of measuring 1/8 inch to 6 inches.

Scoreboards

There are quite a few inexpensive scoreboards that you can find on-line. Most are OK, and many players who are handy with tools create their own. Here are some that I think are worth a look-see.

Tom McNutt of Boccemon.com offers a scoreboard "built with serious Bocce players in mind". The aluminum signboard mounts easily to a 2" pipe, providing "Excellent visibility for players and spectators. Ideal for all weather conditions." McNutt will customize the scoreboard with your own artwork. See www.boccemon.com for more photos and current prices.

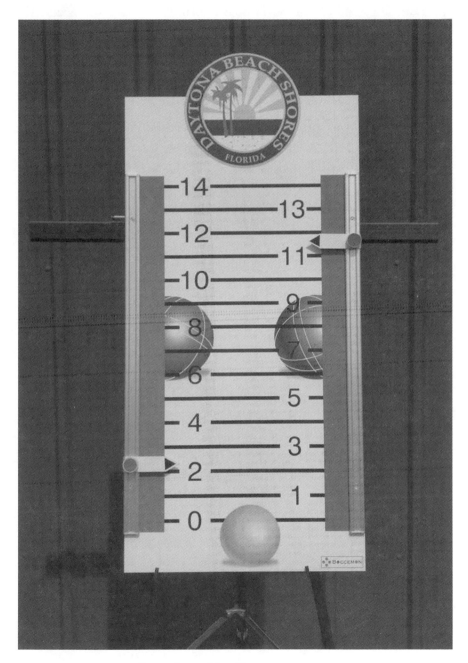

Scoreboard by Boccemon.com

David Brewer of BocceBrew.com offers two scoreboards. One is a "Heavy Gauge Aluminum Score Board with 3M vinyl paint. Magnetic balls travel on a steel rod to keep score. Measures 3' by 10" Comes in Both Horizontal and Vertical Styles."

The other is "Kiln dried redwood with polyurethane coating and 3M vinyl paint. Magnetic balls travel on a steel rod to keep score. Measures 3' long by 10" tall by 3/4" thick."

East Coast bocce promoter Rico Daniele offers two styles of scoreboards. One is 3' by 4' made of heavy duty plastic (fiberglass) and another is metallic that measures 4' by 8'. View them at *http://www. boccebella.com*.

Over the years my bocce posse has created a series of scoreboards. After going through several generations, tweaking the design as we went along, we've settled on one that fits the bill. It is relatively small and lightweight, is reasonably priced, and can be shipped relatively inexpensively. It consists of two basic parts. There is a metal rod that we pound into the ground at half court with a rubber mallet. The scoreboard then slips onto the top (and can be fastened with the turn of a screw). This simple scoreboard can be viewed from both ends of the court making it convenient for when you walk back and forth playing both ends. It also does the trick when you station teammates at each end who play one end only – no walking back and forth. Find more photos and info at JoyofBocce.com.

The double-sided Joy of Bocce scoreboard is placed at half court and can be viewed from both ends of the court.

Court Maintenance Tools

(Get more info on the following products at JoyofBocce.com)

I've seen all kinds of home-made court maintenance brushes and scrapers. Two things have always struck me about them. 1 – They look like they are home-made, and 2 – They tend to be HEAVY.

Drag Brush

Lee Tennis, (makers of the Har-Tru court surface material) is now marketing their tennis court maintenance tools to bocce players. Even though these items were originally created for tennis, they are ideal for bocce. I love their 7-foot drag brush. It is light-weight and, even if you have a 13- or 14-foot wide court, you can smooth it over with just two passes. This is quick enough to do between games without causing much delay. Bristles are 4 ½ inches of synthetic fibers and the strong but light-weight frame is aluminum.

Lute/Scarifier

This handy, light-weight metal rake-like tool is excellent for grooming bocce courts. The 30" wide device is actually two tools in one. It is an all-aluminum combination tool for scarifying, leveling, and removing loose court material. Strong and sturdy, this tool is light enough to handle with ease and is excellent for spreading new material during top-dressing. The concave shape of the 30" wide blade allows the tool to "float" along the surface without digging in. Use the serrated edge to scrape material from high spots, then flip the tool over to rake and smooth that spot and drag the loose material to fill in a lower point. Also available in 48" width.

Aussie Clean Sweep

If you have a problem with leaves on your court this combination tool from Australia helps pick up and remove leaves, pine needles, and pebbles. You pull it like a drag brush, grooming your court as you remove unwanted debris. The PVC tines lift the debris and flip it on top of the unit so it can be carried off the court. Available in 4' and 8' widths.

Portable Bocce Courts

Chris Pfeiffer of Backyard Bocce has developed a clever, portable bocce court. If you like playing on the lawn in a kind of "anything goes" style, you don't need one of these portable courts. But, if you want a little more structure, or maybe want to run a backyard tournament, these ingenious courts are the answer. They are 12' by 60' vinyl boundary template courts that can be set up on grass or dirt.

Set-up is not unlike pitching a tent. You stretch out the template, pull it tight with bungee cords, then drive a couple of stakes into the ground. Next, plant some flags indicating end lines and half court (visual landmarks), and you are set to go within five minutes. Foul lines are demarcated by green and red vinyl sewn into the material ten feet from each end.

Although many of us like longer courts, most Special Olympics bocce (for which the product was originally created) is on 12' by 60' of real estate. The decision to opt for these dimensions is probably a good one for backyard play. I also like the fact that there is just one foul line at each end (10' from the end) rather than one line for hitting and another for pointing. Also, midcourt (30') is clearly marked to indicate minimum distance the pallino must travel to begin each frame.

This product is more a boundary marker than a court. It simply demarcates a 12' by 60' rectangle for play. Any ball that rolls or is knocked out of the rectangle is out of play – a "dead ball."

The courts solve one nagging problem for lawn bocce players. They limit how far left or right a player may move to roll a ball. Sometimes a well played point is right in front of the object ball. To avoid knocking it closer, the opponent gains a better angle by moving a step to the left, then another, then another. Eventually he gets to a point where he is gaining an advantage. With these courts you have to stay in bounds (within the template) to roll each ball.

The courts are ideal for casual, recreation players who want to "step up" a notch without spending big bucks for their own traditional court. Many who host Fourth of July cookouts and other family events include bocce as part of the festivities. Now they can purchase a couple of these courts and offer an organized backyard bocce tournament complete with bracket boards. Anyone can be a tournament director!

With this product, I recommend dropping the wheels on your lawnmower, and cutting the grass before play (at least over the section where you'll place the courts).

Also, sometimes "standard" size pallinos get obscured by the grass. You may want to use a larger target. A croquet or field hockey ball works nicely. In a pinch, use a baseball or any ball about the size of a baseball.

Other Paraphernalia and Novelty Items

As bocce has grown in popularity, an array of unique products has been developed. A computer search will easily turn up all manner of sportswear and apparel, miniature versions of bocce that can be played indoors, and other useful and not so useful devices. You can keep track of new developments by frequenting popular bocce web sites and by subscribing to newsletters like my own *The Joy of Bocce Weekly* (sign up at JoyofBocce.com)

CHAPTER 7

STRATEGY AND TACTICS

S omeone once described bocce as "a game where you throw large balls toward a smaller target ball." That's like saying a fine aged wine is just some old grapes. Bocce involves skill, finesse, strategy, a plan of attack, and the ability to adjust that plan during play. The nuances of play raise it above those games that require only physical skills for success.

Some of the strategies discussed in this chapter are better suited for play on enclosed courts, and others apply more to open area play. The more experience you have playing on different courts and surfaces, the better instincts you will develop for employing the appropriate tactics. Become a student of the game by observing the play of teammates and opponents, especially cagey veterans. If you get "burned" by a particular strategy, file the data in your memory for future reference. Perhaps you can use it to "toast" an opponent sometime down the line. Above all, don't allow yourself to be defeated by the same tactics in the future.

Pre-Game Strategy

In many tournaments, participants play two mock frames (one in each direction) before each game begins. This allows players to get a feel for the surface, and to gauge how the ball is likely to break in one direction or another. Phil Ferrari, of the World Bocce Association, suggests testing the rolling pattern of a court in the following manner. Divide the length of the court in thirds – an imaginary line four feet from each sideboard will create three narrow lanes on a 12-foot wide court. For wider or narrower courts, move your imaginary lines accordingly. Roll as many balls as you are allowed pre-game on all the courts on which you will compete, and watch the glide path. Roll some balls with sufficient speed to make them reach or approach the end board, and make note of any break in their glide path. Remember that a slow moving ball will be more susceptible to this break than a fast moving one. Roll some at different speeds in each of the lanes and note the results. Test out a few bank shots and observe the angle at which the ball comes off the board. Try a few raffa (fast moving) and volo (aerial) shots, if they are in your repertoire (and permitted in the event). Get a feel for the alley and determine what form you are in. Make adjustments.

A longtime coach, I am amazed by the number of intelligent athletes who fail to monitor their game-time performance and make adjustments. As a youth, I played basketball with an exceptional scholar-athlete who possessed a feathery-soft shooting touch. Though he was multi-talented and very bright, he sometimes failed to make critical adjustments. During one game in which he bounced his first half-dozen shots off the front rim, our coach, no rocket scientist, called time out and made a suggestion. "When your shots fall short," he offered, "shoot harder. Try sighting on the back rim." The hooper knocked down most of the rest of his shots, and we went on to win the ball game.

Do all of this practice and adjustment-making on all of your lanes and repeat the procedure from the opposite end of the court. You may want to record your findings in a small notebook. For future reference, you may want to keep a log of all the places you play, but be aware that grooming changes will affect play. Use this pre-game technique every time you play on a court to see if the ball reacts as it did the last time you played there. Some people speak of a court having its own personality and, while home court advantage is a controversial notion in some sports, it's for real in bocce. In social club league games the more talented team generally wins, but the short odds are often on the host team.

The Lineup Card

A good player needs to be skilled in all phases of the game. Every player on the team should be able to point and hit. A player can't be a specialist, competent in only one area. Nevertheless, what follows is our suggestion for filling out your team's lineup card.

In a four-person team, the leadoff player is usually selected for his pointing ability. He or she is the one with the best touch. Some refer to good pointers as six-inchers, implying that no matter where the pallino is, they will usually roll a ball six inches or closer to it. For most of us this is simply wishful thinking. A player able to regularly roll a ball even 12 to 18 inches from the pallino is very skilled.

The number two player is generally chosen for raffa or volo ability. This player can knock away an opponent's point that is too difficult to out-lag (or strike the pallino, sending it to a position more advantageous to his team). The fast rolling ball (raffa) or aerial delivery (volo) is this player's forte.

The number three player is selected for versatility. This player may be called upon to point, or knock away an opponent's ball or the pallino.

Finally, the number four player is the captain. He or she is generally skilled in all shots, has leadership qualities and the people skills not only to set strategy with teammates, but to act as spokesperson in dealings with tournament officials and referees.

Shot Selection

The key in higher levels of bocce competition is not only mastering the techniques of punto, raffa and volo, but knowing when to use each. When the opponents' shot settles in for a good point, sometimes it is better to try to out-lag it, while at other times a knock-away shot is in order. Of course, we have to clarify what we mean by a good point. One foot away (or less) from the pallino is a good point. So is two feet away. A ball two feet in front of the pallino can be a very good point – much better than a ball two feet to the side. A shot even three or four feet away that is in front is always a good point. The other thing to consider when deciding on hitting or pointing is the skill of the player. How good is he at hitting vs. pointing? Think ahead in all situations, asking yourself "What is likely to happen if my shot is successful?" and "What might happen if I miss?" A big factor in the choice of shots is how many balls the other team still has to play. And always bear in mind that any ball, your own or your opponent's, may change the pallino's position. Theoretically, an eight point swing could occur. Four points for their team could become four points for your team with one skillful (or lucky) redirection of the object ball.

Court Surface

The court surface can come into play when deciding strategy and what type of shot to attempt. The kind of surface and its state of grooming need to be considered. Recently groomed courts tend to be faster than those that have been played on for a while. How hard or soft the surface is will affect a volo shot that lands short of its target. Rather than hit and then roll into its target, your volo on a hard packed surface may bounce right over it. This may lead you to select the raffa over the aerial knock-away shot.

Placing the Pallino

One of the crucial strategies in bocce is intelligent placement of the pallino. Having "pallino advantage" gives you the opportunity to go to your team's strengths or to attack your opponents' weaknesses. Of course, a big key is knowing your strong points and their weaknesses. After a few frames, a clever tactical player knows his opponents' weak spots and tries to deliver the pallino there. Rather than pitch or toss the pallino out on the fly, roll it smoothly as if you were pointing. Watch its glide path. Read its motion left or right. Use this information on your following roll(s).

Many players start a frame by tossing the pallino rather willy-nilly, with an overhand, underhand, even between the legs or behind the back delivery. This is fine if you just want to get the round started, and don't care where the target ball ends up or how it got there. But, at a more competitive level, things get a little more cerebral. Remember, having pallino advantage allows you to play to your team's strength or to the opponents' weakness. Similarly, you might be able to avoid the opponents' strong suit. For example, if the other team plays exceptionally well on long rolls, try to place the object ball the minimum distance down court.

Again, roll the object ball in the same manner that you will roll your first bocce ball and from the same spot. Moreover, carefully track the pallino's path, making note of any movement before it comes to rest. When you roll the pallino hold a bocce ball in your other hand so that you can keep the same foot placement and roll that ball exactly as you did the target ball.

Note: Some players, when trying to out-lag an opponent's ball, like to have a ball in each hand. This is for balance, and so feet placement can be maintained if the first attempt is unsuccessful. Instead of missing a shot, turning around to collect another ball for the next roll, then re-establishing a starting position, etc., you are already set to go. This is not allowed in international play. All balls must be in the ball rack except for the one in the hand of the person who is about to roll. This makes it easier for players and referees to see how many balls are still to be played (just check the rack).

If the target ball "fell" to the right as it rolled down the court, you can start your bocce ball out a little more to the left to compensate. (Note: some recommend that when a court's surface has variations that influence the roll of a ball, players should move their starting point in the direction that the ball falls.)

Let the pallino come to rest, then try to establish the initial point by rolling your first ball as close as possible to that target – in front (a tad short) is always better than long and/or left or right of it. When the point is in front of the object ball it provides "nuisance value" as opponents have to negotiate around the ball and may inadvertently tap it closer to the pallino.

If you are partial to bank shots, you may want to aim the pallino close to a sideboard. But be aware that a point that is close to the pallino, but up against the sideboard, is a relatively easy target. A smart player will make a nice transfer of energy shot, hitting your ball away and leaving his in its place. If your opponents are expert at bank shots, you may want to place the object ball in the open court where they will not attempt rebound shots. The problem with spending time perfecting bank shots is that when you travel to other courts, the boards don't always respond predictably. Also, if you aspire to international style play, bank shots are not allowed.

The First Roll – Initial Point

While it is customary for the person who tossed the pallino to roll the first ball, in high levels of play it is often the captain who places the object ball. He then stands aside as his point man sets the initial point. According to highly regarded US player Dr. Angel Cordano, "At international level the pallino can be tossed by anyone and usually it is the best player who does it, to assure the position that's most advantageous for the team."

While accurate hitting is extremely important, and versatility is a necessity, rolling for point is the critical skill in bocce. After all, the game evolved from the basic contest of two people trying to outdo each other tossing balls toward a target. If there were a big league bocce draft, great pointers would go in the first round. A player whose shots consistently cozy up to the pallino is in very high demand.

On the first roll establishing the initial point, you have been very successful if it takes your opponent two balls to beat it. If it takes the opposition three or four balls to outlag or knock your ball out of contention, you have been extremely successful, and your team should win the frame. The more balls your opponent uses in his attempt to outdo your initial roll, the better your chance of taking the last shot of the frame. Many players consider the first and second rolls the most critical ones since they will have an impact on who will play the last ball. When you get the last shot (the *hammer*, as some players call it), you have an opportunity to win the frame. Big time college basketball coaches preach the philosophy of working hard to stay in the game so that in the final seconds, their team has a chance to win. That's the goal – to have the opportunity to win the game, even if it is with the last possession. Forcing your opponent to use several balls to beat your initial roll increases your chance of having the hammer. Possessing the hammer gives you the opportunity to win.

Most players like to leave the initial point a tad short rather than long. This presents problems for the opponent, as he must navigate around it, and might even inadvertently bump it closer to the target.

Leaving your initial point in front is also good news for your hitter in case your point gets out-lagged by the opponents. Your hitter doesn't have to be concerned about his ball or the ball he strikes ricocheting into, and displacing, your initial point. Let's say your ball is 18 inches in front, and they close in to 15 inches left of the pallino. A successful hit on their ball will not interfere with the position of your initial point.

When pointing, we recommend the smooth release generating the 12 o'clock to 6 o'clock rotation that we discussed in Chapter 4. Make it your goal to place your initial point so close to the pallino that your opponent needs two, three, or even four balls to beat it.

Subsequent Rolls

"Go to school" on subsequent rolls by you, your teammates or your opponents. Don't wander off, physically or mentally. Don't think about your next shot. Pay attention and read the path of the shots that every player takes in your game. Does a ball fall in a certain direction? How does a player adjust to a bad roll? Does the adjustment work? Does the player hit the sideboard too early or too late on a bank shot? Where do players stand when making a delivery – what angles do they get? Is the angle advantageous, or would another approach be better?

Moving the Pallino to Gain Advantage

There is a version of bocce that uses a large washer as the target. The object of the game is the same – score points by directing balls closer to the target than your opponent can. The difference, of course, is that the target will remain stationary. Its place at the start of the frame will be its position at the end of the frame. But in more conventional bocce using a pallino as the target, attempting to relocate the target ball adds another dimension of strategy. Since the position of the pallino may change at any time during a frame, players need to stay mindful of this. This should be both an offensive and defensive mindset. You need to consider "Where can I redirect the pallino to gain advantage?" and "Where might my opponent try to send the pallino, and how can I prevent or minimize my disadvantage?" Often this simply means keeping a ball near the end-board to prevent the other team from scoring easy points by knocking the object ball there.

"Reading the Green"

In the same area of the court, if a rolling ball falls or breaks to the left from one end, chances are it will fall to the right from the other end. A good player needs to accurately read this break and make adjustments.

When a ball falls or breaks in one direction, players tend to compensate for the break on subsequent shots. Instead of aiming at the target, they sight on a spot that, provided they get the same amount of break, will bring their ball into scoring position. This may or may not be successful. The court surface may crown or peak, and compensating by changing your aim on the next ball may surprise you. You may find it breaking in the opposite direction because it fell off the other side of the crown. For example, you take a smooth roll for point but the ball breaks twelve inches to the right preventing you from closing in for the point. You aim your next shot twelve inches farther to the left, hoping to curve this ball in to the pallino. To your surprise, this time the ball falls off to the left, still leaving your opponent with the nearest ball. When a ball's glide path is near the crown of a court surface, the direction of fall might be unpredictable. The best strategy: when a ball falls in one direction, players must adjust their position on the foul line. Move in the direction that the ball falls. Use the same glide path as on the previous shot, changing only your initial delivery point. If the ball falls right, move your body a step or two to the right. If the ball falls left, move to the left. This is the safest, most consistent strategy. The alternative, staying in the same position but changing the ball's path, can be effective if you have *court knowledge* (experience on the court's surface).

Taking a Chance vs. Playing Safe

Sometimes you need to talk things over with your teammate.

There is an element of risk in many shots that you take in a bocce game. For example, if you attempt a raffa and hit your own ball by mistake, you may help your opponent. If you play it safe, and try to out-lag your opponent's ball, you may not score, but you minimize the damage. Which is the better option? That is a great question, and one for which I have a great answer. It depends. A player needs to take into consideration a host of factors. The score and the situation are critical to making a sound decision on strategy. When you are ahead and cruising toward a sure victory, you tend to get aggressive and "go for it." Being behind in the score and hoping to sneak back into the game might call for a more conservative approach. Late in the game you should consider – if successful, will this one daring play win the game? Has your opponent been surging in the last few frames? If the game goes to another frame, is the other team likely to take the victory? In the end, trust your instincts, make the play and, successful or not, don't second guess yourself. Trust that you made an intelligent decision based on the evidence you had at the time.

"Selling" the Point

Sometimes a shot doesn't turn out the way a player intended. Instead of coming in for a point, the shot bumps an opponent's ball into scoring position, or knocks his own team's point out of contention. It may even move the pallino toward the opponent's ball(s) giving away the point(s). This is "selling" the point, a colorful phrase that depicts one of the most disheartening happenings in the game of bocce. You've become a "salesman" (or "salesperson" for the politically correct). If you play enough, it will happen to you. Deal with it.

Taking a Stand

One kind of tactical bocce is often overlooked. Players often give little thought to selecting the best starting position for an approach or delivery. A 10- or 12-foot court gives you a lot of options. You can legally start your approach anywhere along that 10- or 12-foot width. Walk along that line and check out the view. How much of the pallino do you see from different positions? Play the shot in your mind from the different angles and select the position that gives you the best percentage of being successful. Imagine that the shot ends up exactly as you hope it will. What will your opponents' options be then? Think ahead, then execute.

Sometimes moving to one side or another of the foul line opens up the target zone. For example, in some cases it may be advantageous to knock away your opponent's ball or the pallino. Since you aren't too concerned with which one you hit, move along the foul line to find the launch site that affords you the widest target zone. Whenever you are considering hitting, take into consideration the positions of any balls around your target. What is likely to happen if your shot is off and it hits one of them? How much risk is involved?

Tactical Bocce — Blocking

Many players like to close off the opponents' angle by leaving a ball short of the pallino, or strategically placing a ball to make their attempt more difficult. This concept of blocking an opponent is really playing defense. "Put some pants on it," say shuffleboard players, encouraging a teammate to place a protective block on a well-positioned point. Sometimes a block is used to concede a point, while preventing the opposition from scoring multiple points. Often, players opt for laying their last ball in front. It blocks. It defends. It has nuisance value. It gives the opposition something to think about, and often limits their options.

The referee indicates how far away the opponent's ball is from the target. This knowledge will help you on your next roll.

A good defensive mindset is to concentrate on never allowing your opponents to score multiple points. A big score by the opposition boosts their confidence and puts added pressure on your team. Stay in the game by avoiding giving up two-, three- and four-point rounds.

Hit Early, Point Late

If you are debating whether to close in for point or hit your opponent's ball away, consider the following. If you are going to hit, do it first. Your point attempt might be short, and could possibly block your path to the target on subsequent attempts. Like billiards, you want to "see" the object in order to hit it. So hit early, point late. If you miss with the raffa or volo attempt, you can then decide to close in or try another hit. Teams may try to hit twice in a row, but usually not three times. If it is 11 o'clock (one point away from defeat in a twelve-point game) a team may try a third consecutive knock-away shot to save the game.

Consider this scenario: in a doubles match your opponents roll the pallino out and then place a close point requiring your team to hit. Your hit attempt misses and you decide to try a second hit. You might be inclined to say to your teammate, "Why don't you try it this time?" But the percentages are better if the same person attempts both hits. He can adjust by analyzing just how he missed the first try and, should he miss again, his teammate will have two chances to "close in" and "minimize the damage." This makes for better odds than two players each having one ball to lag.

Many good players like to hit an opponent's ball away, even if it isn't extremely close. As we pointed out in Chapter 5, players want to have a ball near the backboard as a kind of insurance against the pallino being knocked there later in the game. So, the knock-away shot presents a win-win situation. It serves its team well either by hitting its target, or rolling to the backboard.

When your team has three balls to play and your opponent has but one, hitting is a good option. For example, you establish the initial point with a roll 10 inches from the object ball. Your opponents try to hit your ball away and miss. They attempt to hit again and miss. Next they point and close in to eight inches from the pallino. They have one ball left, you have three. Since they are in, it is your turn. Hitting is a good option in this situation, even if you feel you can close in, because you want their ball out of there. If it stays, it's going to be a nuisance, perhaps even preventing you from scoring big. If you miss, you still have two balls to try to close in for point or hit (you make the call!).

Not Only What, But Who?

An important strategic consideration is not only what strategy to attempt, but which player should execute the task. You might consider who is more skilled at the particular type of shot, and who feels more confident about getting the job done. Another consideration is how many balls are left for each player to roll. For example, your team has three balls left to play, the other team has none. Your opponents are in for one point. You decide to hit. One player on your team has two balls to roll, and the other has one. The player with one ball left should attempt the hit. If he misses, his partner will still have two chances to close in for point. If he is short or long on the first attempt, he can adjust with the second ball and should win the frame. Had the player with two bocce balls attempted the hit and failed, he and his partner would then each have one chance to close in. The percentages, however, favor one player with two chances over two players with one chance each.

The Polaroid Approach and Positive Mental Imaging

In Chapter 4, we introduced what I'll call the Polaroid approach. Stand near the backboard and take a mental Polaroid, pause to let it come into focus, then block everything out and focus on the shot. Before executing, create a positive mental image of a well-placed shot. Get your teammates to avoid comments that create a negative image. "Don't be short of the pallino" gives an image of a shot that doesn't quite reach its intended destination. "Make it reach beyond the pallino" creates a different picture in the mind. The body aspires to the mental images it processes. We teach our baseball players not to say things like "Don't lose 'em!" when the pitcher gets behind in the count. We want to hear encouragement that produces positive images. "Throw strikes, big guy!"

or "Toss it right down the middle of the plate, Mark!" are comments we want to hear and they create the images we want to visualize.

There is a great deal of documentation supporting mental imagery as a valid tool for improving skills in basketball, football, swimming, karate, skiing, volleyball, tennis and golf. There is no reason it can't help your bocce game. When attempting a roll with the game on the line, consider this three-step approach (thanks to Dr. Angel Cordano).

1. Take a deep breath.
2. Visualize the best shot you ever made.
3. Execute the shot with confidence.

CHAPTER 8

BUILDING A BACKYARD COURT

You can have a great deal of enjoyment playing bocce without a professional-looking court on your premises, and thereby preserve your open space for other activities. One of the most attractive aspects of the sport has always been that it can be played by anyone almost anywhere. If you do opt for a court enclosed by sideboards and end boards, it is likely to be a permanent structure. The task of building a quality court is not to be taken lightly. To construct anything but the simplest of bocce courts, your yard is going to be in a state of disarray for weeks. Your lawn will likely be devastated by trucks delivering gravel, stone dust or clay, and your relationship with significant others may be altered. You also need to consider the effect the court's construction will have on the neighborhood. Will it be a welcome sight or an eyesore? Is there a chance that you'll someday put up spotlights for night play? How will this affect the neighborhood's tranquility?

The Building Site

Once you've made the decision to build a court, spend some time deciding on its precise location. Side yard or backyard? Are there trees and shrubs that will have to be sacrificed? How does the land pitch from one end to the other? Where can you build that allows you to create the court that meets the dimensions you desire? Is one area more conducive to good drainage than another? Soil types and drainage patterns vary widely from one area to another (you can install perforated pipe to aid drainage). How will sunrise and sunset affect play? Some builders recommend that the court's length run north to south to prevent annoying glare at dawn and dusk.

The final site should be the rectangular piece of your property that comes closest to satisfying the above issues. You may have to make trade-offs. The most level area available to you may not be the most esthetically pleasing or the most convenient location. You may have to sacrifice or relocate favored trees or shrubs.

My family home is on a corner lot in a pleasant, family neighborhood. We debated the merits of building the court on our side yard (surrounded by a four-foot tall, split picket fence) vs. our backyard (enclosed by a six-foot chain link fence). We finally opted for the privacy afforded by the backyard, which also preserved our side yard's open space for other activities like volleyball, badminton, and bocce on the lawn. I had hoped for a 76- by 12-foot court, but settled for 76 by 10 because I wasn't willing to sacrifice a row of fruit trees that border the playing area. The compromise worked well as the line of trees gives a European ambiance to our court.

The Dimensions

People always ask if a court is regulation or "official" size. The question is difficult to answer because different governing bodies mandate different court dimensions. Here on the East Coast there are many 60- by 12-foot courts, built to International Bocce Association standards, (a group that is now defunct). However, organizations in other areas prefer larger courts of 70 to 90 feet in length. True international court dimensions are 27.5 by 4 meters for volo play, and 26.5 by 3.8 to 4.5 for punto raffa volo competition. (We discuss these styles of play in Chapter 11, International Play). So, if you want a court that meets these specifications, you'll want one that is approximately 90 feet long by 13 feet wide.

You can build a court of any length and width that you desire, unless you plan to host a tournament. That tournament court will have to meet the specifications outlined in the governing body's rules. As we have stated, there are courts as short as 60 feet and as long as 90 feet or more. Widths run anywhere from eight feet to 14 feet or more. Another thing to factor into your decision is the cost. The bigger the court, the greater the cost is for materials and construction (also, the greater the expense and effort to maintain).

How Long?

Many veteran players don't like the 60-foot courts, maintaining that they are too short and provide too small a playing area. Many rules require the initial toss of the pallino to come to rest on or beyond the half court marker (30 feet). Since a player may hit from the 10-foot line, a target near midcourt may be as close as twenty feet away. Compounding the problem is that in many local tournaments, players get away with flagrantly violating the foul line. Their approach and delivery bring them practically on top of the ball they're trying to hit. Many bocce players prefer longer courts (in the 70 to 76 foot range). This seems a good compromise between the 60 and 90 foot extremes. You have enough open court to make for challenging play, and the size is reasonable for a family's backyard.

How Wide?

Courts are as narrow as eight feet (or less) and as wide as 14 feet (or more). Widening the court minimizes the luck factor and maximizes the need for skillful play. For example, picture a court eight feet wide with the pallino resting at one end right in the center of that width. Considering only the width, the worst possible shot a player could make will end up no more than about four feet to the left or right of the target. A wider court means more open space calling for more precise rolling. Ten to twelve feet is a reasonable width.

To make your decision on court dimensions, take all of the foregoing into consideration. Keep in mind the difference between a court for backyard, recreational use and one for league or international tournament play. If you want to represent your country in international play, construct the large court. Otherwise, build it to fit your situation, your yard, and your pocketbook. Most of all, build the court that makes you happy. If you only have room for a small court, fine! Build it and enjoy it. Don't let the court's size diminish the joy of playing. My good friend Del Bracci of Bradford, Massachusetts had only enough room on the side of his house for a 9' by 45' stone dust court. This "derringer" of a court was nothing but a source of great enjoyment for Bracci and the host of players who competed there.

Another Trade-Off

Before we built our court, we played exclusively on our grassy, side yard and became pretty good players. When we entered tournaments played on stone dust or clay courts, however, we regularly got trounced. Several months after completing our court, my son James and I competed in a tournament in Old Lyme, Connecticut on 76- by 12-foot courts. We played pretty well, winning several matches and competing well in those that we lost. The backyard court clearly helped us get to the next level. But it's somewhat disturbing that we don't seem to play on the lawn any more. Lawn bocce is a wonderful game full of challenging natural obstacles. While in Connecticut for the above-mentioned tournament, we visited friends from the Special Olympics Bocce Committee at the home of Roger Lord. After a delightful cook-out and reunion, we played lawn bocce. Roger has a world-class bocce lawn. The course has rolling hills and level areas and is a delight to play on. You need to be able to roll oh, so gently downhill and sometimes you have to heave the ball volo-like uphill. And you have to read the green like a golfer on the PGA tour. I had almost forgotten how much joy good friends and good lawn bocce could provide. Building a backyard court brings with it this trade-off. You are going to get better at competitive tournament-style bocce, but you are probably not going to play much on the lawn again.

Initial Grading

Once you have the site and court dimensions selected, stake out the area using wooden stakes and mason's line. The staked area should be slightly larger than the finished playing area to allow access for heavy equipment. You'll need to strip the entire area of sod and loam, probably digging up and removing 12 inches of material. Grading with a bulldozer, Bobcat, or front-end loader may be necessary. The final playing surface must be as level as possible to provide for the best possible playing conditions. Some suggest treating the stripped area with herbicide or putting down rolls of plastic landscape fabric to prevent new growth of grass or weeds coming up through the court surface.

Sideboards, Squaring the Court, Leveling the Boards

Once the playing area is stripped, reset the stakes to the precise play area measurements. Put up the sideboards now, using a transit, carpenter's level, or line level. Leaving one end-board until last allows for easy access for a wheelbarrow or machinery to deliver and spread materials. The side and end-boards may be of any material that will not move when struck by a ball. They must be at least as high as the balls (6 to 12 inches recommended). Both ends can be higher to protect spectators and players because most balls knocked out of the court exit near the ends. You can construct the court walls with landscaping timbers (6" x 6" or 8" x 8"), or wood planking. Pressure treated stock is recommended. Note: Some courts are built with concrete around the perimeter and then lined on the inside with pressure treated wood. According to the United States Bocce Federation, this promotes "billiard-like accuracy for balls rebounding off the side walls." Be sure to square the ends of the boards before installing them. To square the court, measure the diagonal distance between the corner stakes. The lengths should be equal. Use a transit to mark the stakes at the appropriate height and secure the line tightly at these marks. For example, if you are using 12-inch high sideboards, mark one stake 12 inches from the subsurface and shoot your transit readings from that mark. Without a transit, use the longest level you can obtain and, instead of marking the stakes, set one sideboard in place at a time using the mason line and leveling as you go along. Remember, save one of the end-boards for last. Set the other side of the court along the mason's line, leveling it relative to the first side. Use a board long enough to reach across the width of the court for this job, reading the carpenter's level that is placed on top. Drive stakes two to three feet into the ground to shore up the boards and keep them straight. Use the mason's line to guide your work on the sideboards.

Some builders recommend steel reinforcing rods 5/8" in diameter by 24" long if the side walls are three inches or thicker. The idea is to drill holes vertically down through the width of the boards every five or six feet, driving the rods into the ground until they are flush with the top of boards. With two-inch or narrower boards you can use 1" x 24" rods. Drive these into the ground against the sideboards at five- to six-foot intervals and attach with u-bolt clamps. Use no reinforcing rods in the end-boards since they experience the most wear and tear and are the most likely to need repair or replacement. Also, be aware that steel rods used externally will eventually rust.

Note: You may want to drill a small hole through the end-board to allow excessive water to drain after rainstorms. Drill the hole parallel to, and just above the court's surface. This is important if you are running a tournament, and don't have time to wait for your court to dry out naturally.

The Sub-Surface Materials

Some builders recommend a five-inch layer of sand followed by three inches of crushed stone. This will ensure good drainage. Many builders skip the sand and use only gravel or crushed stone as a base. Other than #1 or #2 crushed stone, a gravel mix, or any mixture of pebbles, ground shell, sand, or soil that provides adequate drainage may be used. The USBF recommends three inches of baserock (two inches in diameter) to avoid the risk of gravel or smaller stones ultimately working their way to the surface and creating a rough course. Some builders recommend wetting and compacting the subsurface with a tamper or a gas-driven compactor. Others opt for doing the compacting only when the final surface is in place.

Choosing the Surface Material

A Tale of Three Popular Choices
(Stone Dust, Oyster Shell, Clay)

{With input from Tom McNutt, Michael Grasser, David Brewer, and Mike Esposito, some of the top names in the American bocce court building business.}

Although people use all sorts of different bocce surface materials (grass, indoor/outdoor carpet, synthetic turf), the following three come up most often in court construction conversations. Stone dust, crushed oyster shell, and clay are often referred to as the "Cadillacs" of surface materials.

According to bocce court builder Tom McNutt (boccemon.com), they are the only materials that give you the ability to level the court, maintain it without undue effort, and produce an acceptable "speed to bounce ratio." We want speed but we don't want bounce. If we rated materials on a scale of one to ten, with ten being the optimal score, concrete might score a 10 for speed and a 0 for bounce (it plays fast – that's good, hence 10 - but provides a pretty hefty bounce on a volo attempt – that's bad, hence 0). At the other end of the spectrum we might find that sand scores a 0 for speed and a 10 for bounce (ball doesn't roll so fast, but won't bounce).

Stone dust, oyster shell, and clay produce very acceptable speed/bounce numbers.

Stone Dust

Stone dust is popular because of its exceptional drainage qualities and low cost. It is especially appropriate in New England (where it is easily obtained) and in places that get lots of rain. In some areas, stone dust is known as decomposed granite. On the West Coast, builders refer to it as "quarter stone by dust." Often, stone dust is crushed limestone. Bocce court builder and Michigan landscape architect Mike Grasser prefers crushed limestone, sometimes mixing two or three parts with one part clay for the top 1/8-inch of the court surface.

Grasser also has considerable expertise with artificial surfaces, having traveled extensively in Europe interviewing synthetic bocce court product specialists. "If you opt for carpet," he warns, "check the nap." If carpet fibers don't stand up straight (are not at right angles to the floor), a court is likely to roll faster in one direction than the other. Synthetic turf surfaces are preferable in this regard, as the fibers tend to be short and sturdy.

As far as high end synthetics go, Grasser has experience with surfaces that roll out like linoleum. Most, he maintains, tend to crack or split after a couple years of play. Carpets tend to stretch too, leaving wrinkles and "waves" after a season or two. The best artificial surfaces are poured, self-leveling substances which are popular in European bocce facilities. Developed for indoor, covered courts, the surface can be used outdoors in climates that don't experience frost (and one contractor told me it can work in colder climes too if the poured concrete base is installed properly). Such courts usually include "channel drains" around the perimeter to sweep out surface puddles after rainstorms. As you might expect, these almost maintenance-free courts are among the most expensive on the market.

In the USA, California's Campo di Bocce (Los Gatos and Livermore), Michigan's Palazzo di Bocce, and Illinois' Pinstripes have installed these polyurethane self-leveling surfaces.

Crushed Oyster Shell

The shell of the oyster is very popular on the West Coast where it is readily available. The oyster beds of San Francisco Bay are a popular source. Primarily used to create agricultural by-products for soil fertilization as well as chicken and cattle feed enhancers, oyster shell makes an excellent bocce surface. Tom McNutt prefers this top dressing, and begins with a base of crushed Pacific oyster shell (same stuff you would get by grinding up your oysters on the half shell). These are ¾" and smaller.

Next comes a layer of finer oyster flakes. Finally the court is topped off with very fine oyster flour (a powder used as a soil amendment – farmers or gardeners might use it to return calcium to the soil). McNutt reports that his oyster shell courts are playable even shortly after heavy rains.

Note: Some court builders prefer to mix the oyster shell with clay or crusher fines.

Clay (Har-Tru, Baseball Infield/Warning Track Clay)

Although some bocce court builders use baseball infield clay or warning track clay as a topping, the most appropriate "clay" is really not a clay. Manufactured by Lee Tennis, Har-Tru is sometimes called "American clay" – it's actually crushed metabasalt (very hard, angular volcanic stone). According to New England sales representative Pat Hannsen, "Har-Tru performs better than clay because clay absorbs water and holds it, making the surface unplayable rapidly, while drying out slowly." Har-Tru's product includes gypsum which acts as an initial set-up aid. Once cured, the product plays well and allows excess water to drain by percolating down through the medium.

Har-Tru plays fast and true and has excellent speed/bounce numbers when installed correctly. I put one inch of this product over my stone dust court to "step up" to a faster playing surface. I was a little concerned about drainage, but once it "cured" or "set", it drained quite well (had a heavy rainfall on a Sunday and was able to play our regular Monday morning league as usual).

For a free, no obligation quote on Har-Tru material for your court, visit joyofbocce.com and fill out the Quote Request Form available via the navigation button labeled Har-Tru.

David Brewer of BocceBrew.com tells me...

> "We read your book years ago and it was an inspiration to investigate court design and construction. We have built 65 courts in the last three and a half years, including courts for John Madden, George Lucas, and Headquarters for Yahoo.com, wineries, hotels, restaurants, public parks, retirement communities and private homes."

Like his Pacific Northwest counterpart, Tom McNutt, Brewer favors the readily available oyster shell, using it in a one-to-one mixture with infield clay. "It is very malleable," says Brewer, "making the courts easy to level and maintain." Running a drag brush or broom over the surface makes for quick and easy grooming between games. Water percolates well through oyster shell, and the surface will harden, but not as much as stone dust or Har-Tru. All of the above, combined with the fact that crushed limestone is less readily available on the West Coast, makes oyster shell an outstanding choice.

George C. Scott, playing the boxer's father in the 1979 movie Rocky Marciano, proclaims that "In Italia, a rich man's bocce court – a real bocce court – is made of the crushed shell from the oyster."

Bocce Court Construction

California:
Contact David Brewer at www.boccebrew.com (415-461-8842)

Michigan:
Contact Michael Grasser at DaVinciBocce.com (248-681-9022)

Washington & Pacific Northwest:
Contact Tom McNutt at www.boccemon.com (360-224-2909)

New England:
Contact Mike Esposito via www.JoyofBocce.com (978-686-8679)

The Surface

Finally, after deciding on your surface, spread up to three inches of the material. Another option is to put a one-inch top coat of your material of choice over your existing surface. If you opt for the one-inch topping, some recommend putting it down in four applications of 1/4 inch at a time. Wet and roll the material with a heavy roller between applications. The surface must be dry enough that it doesn't collect on the roller during this process.

Initially, my backyard court was surfaced with three inches of stone dust. We wet and rolled the surface with a heavy roller, repeating the process daily. Playing games in between helps expose the high and low spots. An option is to let the surface settle for a season and then add an inch of either brick dust or fine sifted clay, or Har-Tru top dressing (caution - these may be tracked into the house). I opted for one inch of Har-Tru after a couple years of play, and am very happy with the choice. Plays fast and true – drains well, but not as well as stone dust – cures very hard so that weeds can't take root – drawback = once New England fall weather sets in (freezing and thawing season) we have to shut down until the spring. Water gets locked up as ice in the morning, then melts and the surface becomes soggy as the sun rises and temperatures increase.

Leveling the Surface

Roll the surface with a heavy roller. Wet the surface down, let it dry, and roll again. After the initial rolling process, use an angle iron or a straight board about the width of the court and drag it lengthwise across the court. This scraping process, called screeding by concrete workers, removes high spots and fills in low points. Repeat this screeding process several times, wetting and rolling between each pass. You can also use a rigid rake 30 inches or more in width to scrape and grade the surface. These are sometimes called infield rakes because baseball groundskeepers use them. They have teeth on one side, and a grading surface on the other. The lute/scarifier by Lee Tennis described in the previous chapter (which was developed for tennis court maintenance) is an outstanding tool for bocce court leveling.

Leveling the final surface takes some time and help from Mother Nature in the form of rainfall. A good soaking rainstorm speeds up the leveling process considerably by exposing low spots (puddles) that you can fill with additional material. A galvanized fence post the width of the court can also help with leveling. Set it down across the width of the court and place a four-foot carpenter's level on top of it. Besides the feedback from the level's bubble, low spots and irregularities show up clearly when light passes underneath the bar.

Initially, the surface will be soft enough so that a ball dropped from waist level or above will leave an indentation where it strikes the ground. Over time the surface should get harder and play faster. Volo shots that strike the surface will leave large, round dimples at first. As the court surface becomes harder, the size of the indentations will decrease. These marks may start out the size of a softball on a new court. Eventually, they shrink to the size of a silver dollar, half dollar, and then a quarter. When they approximate the size of a dime, the court is fully hardened.

Swingboard Construction

Use two-by-tens slightly shorter than the court's width as swingboards. At each end of the court, suspend the boards just off the court surface using screw hooks that latch onto eye bolts inserted into the backboard. During play, these swingboards absorb the energy of raffa impacts, thus discouraging rebound attempts off the end-board. Usually, builders cover this board with a material (carpet, rubber, old fire hose) that adds to the "give" of the board and protects it from damage. Other backboard designs are acceptable, but it is essential to have backboards constructed in such a way that they allow only minimal (or no) bounce back.

Extra Height at the Ends

To ensure that balls hit by raffa and volo attempts stay in the court, you can add additional height at the end-boards and sideboards near both ends. You can accomplish this by adding additional tiers or levels of boards. Fasten these boards securely to the existing structure and brace them with wood stakes and/or metal brackets. Use galvanized screws, not nails. You will have to gauge how far out from the end-board to extend this added height (16 feet recommended). Some recommend courts with an interesting staircase effect. The sideboards are one foot high. Starting at 12 feet from the end-board the height of the sides increases to three, four, then five feet high. This increases the cost of construction and might be overkill unless you play with very hard rolling hitters. Also, spectators often struggle to see over the fortress-like planking.

Tools and Materials Needed

- landscaping timbers or planking for side and end-boards (pressure treated)
- steel reinforcing rods or other means for staking boards
- sand
- crushed stone
- surface material (clay, stone dust, or other screened topping)
- heavy machinery (backhoe, Bobcat, etc.)
- pick

- shovel
- rake
- hammer
- sledge hammer
- ax (for tree or root removal)
- transit
- four foot or longer carpenter's level
- line level
- mason's line
- framing square
- 100-foot steel tape measure
- heavy lawn roller
- L-shaped framing brackets and metal tie plates
- screws (not nails) 1½- and 3-inch galvanized decking screws
- 9- or 12-volt battery operated screw gun AC/DC
- circular saw

Court Markings

Depending on whose rules you intend to play by, your court markings will be different. Some groups play with one foul line that is both for pointing and hitting. I recommend this unless you aspire to play by the international rules. On those long courts they use one line for pointing and raffa attempts, one for volo hitting, and another for lofting a raffa the minimum distance on the fly. Many 60-foot courts utilize a foul line for pointing 4' from each backboard, and a foul line for hitting 10' from each backboard. Hopefully, as the game continues to grow, a standard will emerge that will be embraced by all the various groups. The United States Bocce Federation Open Rules reprinted in Chapter 10 are a good step in that direction. The USBF is the governing bocce of bocce in America. The more groups that adopt the USBF Open Rules, the closer we'll get to standardization.

At any rate, foul lines are generally painted on both side boards. You may also want to put down a chalk line on the surface much like a baseball foul line.

For international play, the pointing and raffa line is four meters from the end-board, while the volo line is seven meters from the end. See Chapter 11 for international rules and contact the United States

Bocce Federation (www.Bocce.com) for additional information on international courts and tournament play.

Most rules call for the initial toss of the pallino to come to rest at or beyond midcourt. You will need to paint this line on both sideboards as well. Again, for league or tournament play you may want a chalk line running across the surface.

Finally, many rules call for the first toss of the pallino to come to rest a minimum distance from the backboard (e.g. three or four feet from the backboard). The Open Rules outlined in Chapter 10 are gaining momentum and they contain no such restriction except that the initial toss of the pallino not touch the backboard.

Top Dressing Technique

When our bocce group top dressed my backyard court, we photo-graphically chronicled the progress. I already had a satisfactory surface of stone dust over crushed stone. It played pretty well and drained beautifully (there could be a heavy downpour and a couple hours later my court was playable). Still, we wanted to "step up" to a faster surface like the top bocce players use.

After some research I opted for Har-Tru material, the popular ten-nis court surface that is making inroads into the bocce court market. I added a one-inch top coat of this over the existing stone dust. Somewhat concerned about drainage, the manufacturer and others who owned or played on such courts allayed my fears.

The good people at Lee Tennis in Virginia determined that I'd need about 5 tons of Har-Tru to create a one-inch top coat for my 76' by 10' court. A do-it-yourself project from the get-go, our bocce crew lifted, lugged, laid down, leveled, and landscaped 125 eighty-pound bags of Har-Tru. And it was one "L" of a job! View the pictorial of our efforts posted at JoyofBocce.com.

Materials needed:

* Har-Tru or other top dressing material (manufacturer will calculate how much you need - get a few extra bags to have on hand for repairs)

- one straight 2 by 4 for "screeding" (should be about 6 inches shorter than the width of the court)
- four pieces of strapping (8 feet long or longer)
- transit (and someone who knows how to use it)
- level (at least 4 feet long)
- shovels
- rakes
- tamper
- wheelbarrow
- garden hose or two
- heavy roller
- one crew of workers (willing to work for food and/or beverages)

Procedure:

(The following assumes starting with a relatively level surface over which the top dressing will be placed.)

Place unopened bags of surface material onto or near one end of the court area. Lay two pieces of strapping (actual measurements 1½" by 1") down about one third of the distance from each side board (the eight-foot length running parallel to the length of the court).

Set transit up (properly leveled) at opposite end and carefully level these pieces of strapping - getting a reference point that you can use consistently throughout the job. We placed a yard stick on end right atop the strapping and were able to sight on the stick's calibrations. You may have to dig material out from under the strapping or add more material beneath to level them. Verify the reference point at both ends of each piece of strapping.

Open bags and dump material onto the court starting at the end board and moving down the length of the strapping.

Take the straight two-by-four and "screed" the material. Screeding is a masonry term for leveling concrete by dragging a straight object over it, pulling excess material away, and smoothing out the surface. It takes two people on their knees to maneuver the two-by-four. Use a side-to-side motion as you screed the material toward you – thus, the two-by-four must be about 6 inches shorter than the width of the court.

Set another two pieces of strapping in place starting from the ends of the previously placed pieces. Level these properly and then carefully remove the first two pieces of strapping, filling in the spaces that they leave with new material.

A trowel can be used to smooth over any minor "bumps and bruises."

Continue down the court in this manner…moving the strapping, checking the reference points, leveling, adding top dressing, screeding, and troweling. The person with the trowel may want to place a piece of plywood down to better bear his/her weight while doing the surface "finish work". Also, workers may opt for surgical masks while working in close proximity to the fine particulates of the top dressing.

Once all the material is in place and leveled you must wet it thoroughly. ALL of the material must be wet. On subsequent wetting and rolling sessions, only the surface needs to be moist.

We used a Y connection added to our backyard faucet and got two hoses going at once. Periodically we took "coring samples" with the trowel to see if the bottom-most part of the material was getting wet. The idea is to make sure it is thoroughly wet but not drenched so that it becomes mush.

The material needs to be completely wet so that it can "cure" or "set up" over the next couple days.

Next, roll with a heavy roller and use a tamper to get the edges and corners where the roller doesn't reach. Roll again each day as you wait for the material to "set."

I knew that my Har-Tru bocce court top dressing would play fast and true. But an unexpected bonus is that, once it hardened sufficiently, it was virtually weed free. With my previous stone dust surface, we'd spend time between frames weeding the court (not a major problem, but a nuisance). The only weeds that can take root are around the perimeter (near the sideboards where the heavy roller doesn't quite reach). Use a tamper to address this problem.

Pat Hanssen of Lee Tennis gives us his take on the top dressing process...

> "Once the screenings have been graded and compacted, the court is ready for the Har-Tru surface. Buy four (4) 1 1/4" O.D. steel pipes, 20' in length, and lay them along the two sides at the edge of the court. Get a long heavy board, cut it about 1/2" shorter than the width of the court and attach metal flashing at the ends. This board will slide easily across the pipes (attach two broom handles for easy handling) screeding out the Har-Tru surface to precisely 1 1/4" depth. Dump 10-12 bags in front of screed board, fluff up material with a rake or, lute/scarifier, and spread evenly across the front of the screed. As the board is pulled, one person can redistribute the Har-Tru as needed to fill in high and low spots. As the material runs out, stop and open more bags until the process is complete.
>
> When compacted dry with a hand or power roller (500 - 1200 pounds of compaction preferred), 1" surface depth will have been achieved. Saturate thoroughly, allow the court to set up, and then roll again. Repeat until desired level of compaction is achieved."

Some Interesting Options

You may want to consider spectator benches for your court. They should be placed carefully, considering both the fans' view of the game and their safety. Fewer balls fly out of the court near the center than at the ends, so caution dictates that benches be placed accordingly. It is rarely seen today, but some bocce players install angle boards (45 degrees from each side to the end-board) that can be used for ricochet and carom shots. Others favor a bumper board over a swingboard. This bumper board doesn't swing, but acts as a shock absorber, collecting the energy of a fast moving ball. Still others use a ditch instead of an end-board. If your ball ends up in the ditch, it is dead. Finally, consider leaving a cut-out or removable section somewhere along your sideboards to allow for both handicap access as well as easy entry and exit for your heavy roller.

Synthetic courts may bring the game to yet another level. Not only is there little maintenance involved, but the game becomes very clean. I mean, your hands don't even get dirty. If synthetic surfaces (poured self-leveling surfaces, indoor/outdoor carpet, synthetic turfs) become the rage, and the game flourishes the way aficionados think it will, the sport just might welcome the designer clothes market.

Portable Courts

Free-standing (portable) courts represent still another option. These can be assembled in twenty minutes or so, played on, and then broken down for storage. Portable courts can be set up outdoors on a level patch of grass or earth, or indoors on composition floors like in a school gymnasium. They are used to conduct tournaments in hotels and convention halls. Courts are set up on the hotel's function hall for example, with the room's carpet becoming the playing surface. After the tournament, the courts are dismantled and the venue reverts to its function hall/meeting room status.

Lighting

If you install lights for night play, they need to be high enough that they aren't shining directly in players' eyes. Also, in analyzing their placement you need to take into account what shadows are likely to be cast. Len Hickey of Wilbraham, Massachusetts has great lighting at his court on his business property – tall telephone poles with powerful lights shining down from high above. Len's lights are on a timer, and local high school kids are welcome to hang out there evenings, playing bocce until the lights go out. Good, safe fun!

Court Maintenance

A well-constructed court should pose only a minimal maintenance problem. The court needs to be groomed after use by brooming, rugging (dragging a rug attached to a rope), or otherwise dragging the surface. The broom, rug, or other device used should be at least 24 inches wide. Thirty-six to 48 inches or more would be preferable to allow for the fewest number of passes when grooming. Fewer passes mean less work and fewer seams where material might collect. The 7-foot drag brush from Lee Tennis is easily the best bocce grooming tool (see Chapter 6).

Occasionally you will have to wet and roll the surface. This will be anywhere from once a month to once a week depending on how much use (and rain) your court gets. Be sure to examine the surface right after rainstorms and fill in any low spots. In the spring you may have to do an annual screeding and some realignment of the sideboards. Occasionally an end-board that has taken its share of raffas needs to be repaired or replaced.

If your court has level side boards and end-boards, you can make use of what is called a "screed board." Take a board almost as wide as the court and screw boards to each end so that you can sit the whole thing across the court's width. The boards screwed to the ends of the middle board rest on the sideboards of the court. This puts the bottom of the middle board at the right height to "grade" the new, soft material to the "right height". Use a builder's level (or transit, or water level) to level these boards end to end and side to side.

Court Construction Synopsis

1. Pick the site
2. Decide on dimensions
3. Stake out an area larger than the actual playing area using wooden stakes and mason's line
4. Strip the area of sod and dirt (12 inches)
5. Reset stakes to actual court dimensions
6. Put up sideboards using transit, carpenter's level, or line level, leaving one end board for last
7. Bring in and spread sub-surface materials
8. Bring in and spread surface materials
9. Compact and level surface using the screeding process, raking, wetting, and rolling with heavy roller
10. Add final end board and additional tiers for desired height
11. Install swingboards
12. Paint court markings
13. Revel in the outdoors and the joy of bocce

When the Har-Tru arrives (in either 50-lb. or 80 lb. bags),
it's time to get your bocce posse ready to go to work.

Put the material down and start the screeding process, starting
at one end of the court and moving all the way to the other end.

The Har-Tru material is very fine. Wearing protective masks while working closely with it is a good idea.

Once done, use a garden hose (or two) to thoroughly wet all the material. The top dressing will "cure" or "set up" over the next few days.

CHAPTER 9

BOCCE COURTS WE'VE KNOWN AND LOVED

What follows is a bocce court pictorial. The photos start on the East Coast and head south, then west, ending up on the Pacific Northwest. Some courts are in people's back yards while others are in the public domain. I hope they provide a basic idea of the almost endless possibilities for enjoying this great game while playing on courts.

Home court of Larry Casha. Andover, Massachusetts.
The court is 70' by 10' with a Har-Tru surface, recessed
string lighting on the side boards, and white vinyl
pergolas on both ends. Photo by Kevin McDevitt.

This 84' by 14' Har-Tru surfaced and lighted court is at
the home of Tom Grella in Methuen, Massachusetts.

Three Har-Tru surfaced courts in the North End
of Boston, Massachusetts. The stone embankments
seemingly invite passersby to take a seat and watch. (Then
we get them to step onto the courts and play).

Home court of Carmine D'Agostino in Franklin,
Massachusetts. The 76' by 12' court has a stone
dust surface and lights for night-time play.

Ralph Bagarella's 72' by 14' Har-Tru surfaced court with night
lighting, music, tv and a beautiful fire pit. Court nestled
within beautiful oak trees in Salem, New Hampshire.

Backyard court at the home of Bob DiTursi in Barrington, New Hampshire. Court is 72' by 10' and top dressed with fine stone dust.

Kathy Flynn photo of the bocce court at Alyson's Orchard in Walpole, New Hampshire. Kathy says you can "point and pick all during one visit."

Wethersfield, Connecticut courts in the public domain at
Millwoods Park. Funds to build the 72' by 12' courts were raised
by UNICO members by selling commemorative bricks on the
walkway between the two courts. Photo by Michael Fortunato.

Two 60' by 12' courts at Honey Brook Borough Park (Pennsylvania).
Libby Nixdorf photo.

Courts at the Mohawk House (restaurant and
function facilities) in Sparta, New Jersey.

Eight courts in the public domain in Colonial Park,
Franklin Township, New Jersey (home of the New Jersey
Bocce Invitational). Photo courtesy of Frank Valanzola.

Pete Chimento's home court in Millstone Township, New Jersey. The 60' by 12' lighted court features a synthetic turf.

George Danner photo of two beautiful grass courts at the Griffin Country Club (Georgia).

Altamonte Springs, Florida. Two Har-Tru surfaced courts
in the public domain located at Westmonte Recreation
Park. Photo courtesy of Sandy McClelland.

Golden Isles Tennis & Bocce Complex in Hallandale,
Florida features three 78' by 13' courts with a 70%
- 30% fine red clay & Florida stone dust mix.

Two nifty 70' by 12' courts just off the beach in Hallandale, Florida.

Six courts at the John Pirelli Lodge #1633 in Beaver
Creek, Ohio. Courts are 60' by 12' and surface
is AstroTurf®. Photo by Gene Kenyo.

Buzzard Hollow Court. Fred Wilburn's 91' by 13' crushed limestone top dressed court in Johnson County, Kansas.

Michael J. Constantini photo of "our courts in Iron Mountain, Michigan (Upper Peninsula of Michigan). The official name is 'The Ray Mariucci Bocce Courts @ City Park'." The six courts are 64' by 11' with limestone/clay top dressing.

Charles G. Apuan's home court in Las Cruces, New Mexico.

Lighted courts at the Italian-American Club of Phoenix,
Arizona. Both ends covered for shelter from the elements.
Photo by Nick Gelormini.

Lincoln Village Townhouse Association in Willow Glen which is a western section of San Jose, California. Richard Boyce photo—90' by 13' court features an oyster flour top dressing.

John Anderson photo shows off his 70' by 8' home court in Salinas, California. Top dressing is decomposed granite. Note the 1700's Burmese temple bell at mid court used to ring out the points scored each frame.

Marin Bocce at San Rafael, California. Photo by Richard
Heisler who says "The San Rafael facility is in a beautiful
setting, just across the Golden Gate from San Francisco and
across the Richmond Bridge from Berkley/Oakland."

Gary Arnstein photo showing his home court in San Anselmo,
California. Court is 60' by 13 ' with oyster shell and clay
surface topped with oyster flour. Arnstein house in the
background designed by a student of Frank Lloyd Wright.

Bill Wallace's 60' by 10' oyster shell and clay court
in Western Sonoma County, California.

Penngrove, California court by BocceBrew.com. The 80' X 12'
oyster shell court has a border made of ipe wood from Brazil.

Sky Park in Scotts Valley, California.
Photo by Dave Wilson.

Sebastopol, California court built by David Brewer (BocceBrew.
com). The 60' by 10' court features a decomposed granite surface.

Another David Brewer court in Ross, California. This one is 60' by 10' with an oyster shell top dressing.

Two courts under pergolas at the Garré Vineyard & Winery in Livermore, California.

Tom Walsh's court in Scotts Valley, California.

Lou Ures' 80' by 11' Forest Court in Florence, Oregon.
It features a crushed oyster shell topping.

Mercer Island, Washington. Photo by landscape designer Kevin Fletcher who was able to fit the 50' by 7' court expertly into the space available. Top dressing is Tom "Boccemon" McNutt's Rain Country Blend.

CHAPTER 10

TOURNAMENT PLAY AND USBF OPEN RULES

Advancing to the tournament level carries with it a trade-off. You gain the more serious competition that you may desire, but you lose the easy, relaxed atmosphere of play in your backyard, neighborhood park, or the beach. Where there was no pressure, no spectators lining the court, no prize money on the line, there is now a whole different ball game.

With a little research, you can probably find some friendly tournament action, but there is also a good deal of high-level (some might even call it cutthroat) competition. The spectrum runs from those like the low-key "Play for the Prosciutto" tourney in Leominster, Massachusetts to those requiring hundreds of dollars for entry fee and big money prizes for the winners. It's probably a good idea to start at the "Prosciutto level" and advance as your skills improve. Many local tournaments feature a relaxed atmosphere with good-natured competition. The players referee their own games, only summoning a tournament official in case of a close measurement or other dispute.

Before you enter a tournament, you should find out certain facts. Call the tournament director, or send for the tourney flier. You'll need to know the tournament format. Is it single elimination (one loss and you're out) or double (two losses)? Is the event for singles, doubles, triples, or four-person teams? If it is for four-player teams, do the players throw two balls each and stay at one end of the court, or do they play one ball each, and play both ends? Can you bring an additional player to serve as a substitute? What is the winning score in each game...12, 15, 16? On what type surface will the event be played--stone dust,

Har-Tru, carpet (some tournaments are run in hotels with temporary courts set up right on the wall-to-wall carpeting)? Will the games be indoors or outdoors? What are the dates and rain dates, if any? Is there prize money (tournament purses are mushrooming as bocce gains in popularity)? If so, how many teams finish "in the money?" How many games do you have to win to make it to the "money round?"

Many local tournaments return virtually all of the money collected from entry fees as prize money. They rely on the bar and concession sales to turn a profit.

As you can see, you are going to have to adjust to different court surfaces and other situations to make it on the tourney circuit. Once you get the details and decide to enter a tournament, you'll have to line up teammates and send in your application and entry fee. If you have a substitute (a fifth player on a four-member team) the captain must decide who plays in which game(s). Most tournament team captains recommend playing the best players in the early games, using the substitute later. The hope is that the stronger team will keep them out of the losers' bracket as long as possible. When you drop out of the winners' bracket early in a double elimination tourney, it makes it very tough to finish in the money.

Probably the most important question you'll need answered is "What rules will govern the tournament's play?" Generally, the game is played the same way in close geographical areas. It is when you travel to another area that problems are likely to arise. A social club hosting a tournament will use its version of the game as the "official" tournament rules, and there may be any number of "house rules". The winning score, for example, may be 11, 12, 15, 16 or more.

In some areas, international rules are observed. Increasingly, we are seeing tournaments governed by "open rules." These are modified from international rules, eliminating some of the restrictions that complicate and slow the game down. Strict international play calls for marking the positions of balls. The player must call his shot when hitting and, if he misses his target, any scattered balls may be returned to their original positions. Open rules are rapidly gaining popularity. And though one group's idea of open rules might be slightly different from another's, they are very similar.

A Tale of Open Rules

The bocce game generally played in North America is very different from the game played in the rest of the world (which is governed by international rules). International rules are well codified and standardized for two games – 1) punto, raffa, volo and 2) volo. As described in Chapter 11, international rules play essentially removes the element of luck from bocce. An errant shot often results in balls being returned to their previous positions. Although groups like the US Bocce Federation vigorously promote both international and open rules, the open rules are much more widely accepted in the USA.

The problem is that there are many differing sets of open rules. None require marking every ball's position, but all vary in subtle and not-so-subtle ways. Some served a good purpose in their day, but failed to evolve as the game matured on this continent. For bocce to get to the next level, we need to adopt international rules, or accept a standardized set of open rules, or both.

First off, when you play at your home or local league, play by any rules you like. Hey, the game is supposed to be fun. Whatever makes the game interesting and exciting for you should be the format you embrace. Play the backboard live or dead, use 45 degree angle boards, make the winning score 21, mandate that you must win by two points, put in a "skunk" or "mercy" rule.

There is an undeniable charm to playing the "house rules" at the home team's venue. They'll play by your rules when they visit your court. But, if you run a tournament, we hope you'll consider United States Bocce Federation Open Rules (reprinted later in this chapter). The USBF is the governing body of bocce in America.

I agree with world-class player Dr. Angel Cordano who says, "I'd like the rules standardized so that we all play the same way, but I'll play any way at all - I just love to play."

All sports go through a period of evolution and the governing rules do too. When I brag to "young pups" about what a good college baseball player I was, they chide me with "Weren't those the days when it was an out if you caught the ball on the first hop?"

Things change. Sometimes they get better, sometimes worse. I hope that the USBF Open Rules reprinted in this chapter represent the next step in the evolution of bocce rules in America.

Suggestions for Anyone Running a Tournament

If you have enough courts, consider reserving one for spectators to give the game a try. Have a charismatic person or two from your group "work the court," coaxing people to step up and attempt a couple rolls. Often there are passers-by or onlookers who, given a little encouragement, would love to give the game a whirl. Make your tournament an opportunity to promote the game.

Suggestion #2 – If we want to compete well with the best teams in the world, we need to promote the international game. As players are exposed to the game, some will aspire to compete internationally. We can help identify those players and point them in the right direction. Set aside 20-30 minutes or so for a demonstration of international play. Contact the USBF to find out who in your area might be available to act as "ambassadors of the international game." If possible, cover his/her expenses for the day.

Perhaps these ambassadors could play an exhibition game, explaining their moves as the contest progresses.

United States Bocce Federation
Open Rules
Revised 2011

Reprinted with permission
Visit the USBF website @ www.Bocce.com for updates

The United States Bocce Federation is a nonprofit, charitable corporation organized to promote the sport of Bocce through education and amateur competition and any funds received are used strictly for this objective. The USBF is the only internationally sanctioned governing body for Bocce in the United States. The USBF is also a member of the Federation International de Boules and the Confederazione Boccistica Internazionale.

THE EVOLUTION OF RULES

Who can play Bocce?

Everyone can play! There is no race, sex, or age discrimination in the sport of Bocce. It is played all over the world and is part of the International Special Olympics and the Senior Olympics.

What do you need to play?

You need a set of eight balls, four for each team, with different colors and a target ball called a "jack" or "pallino". It is also helpful to have some type of measuring device. Tape measures are commonly used as well as antennae, expanding pens, etc.

How many people on a Team?

Games can be played one-on-one (singles), pairs (doubles), triples, or foursomes. In USBF format, singles are played with each person throwing 4 balls and alternating use of each end of the court. In doubles (pairs), each team member throws 2 balls and again alternate use of each end of the court. Triples has become the newest format and 12 balls are used instead of 8. Play is the same as Doubles with each team member throwing 2 balls and alternating use of each end of the court. Foursomes should be played with 2 members of a team stationed at opposite ends of the court and playing 2 balls each. Variations to the foursome style are used in some regions of the USA and certainly are permissible and at the discretion of Tournament Directors or organizers.

Court Dimensions:

Official courts are 86.92' in length and 13.12' in width. Unofficial courts can be smaller. Court surface has the greatest variation found in the USA. Some examples are: carpet, crushed stone, dirt, oyster shells, clay, and most recently synthetic carpets and poured liquid creating a smooth, extremely fast surface.

Ball Size:

The USBF recommends for tournament play: 107 mm Diameter and

920 grams (approx 2 lbs) in weight. Usually Tournament Directors will announce if only "house balls" can be used. The USBF allows players to use their own set as long as the specifications are approved prior to the start of the games.

Foul Lines:

- Should be clearly marked both on court surface and side boards.
- There should only be one line for pointing and shooting and the recommendation is 13' from the back wall.

Players may step on but not have their foot completely over the foul line before releasing the pallino or the bocce ball.

Start the Game!

Begin the game with a flip of a coin between the Captains of each team. The winner of the coin flip will determine the end from which play will start and also has control of the pallino. The losing team chooses the color of balls it wants to use (applies when "house" balls are used). Coin toss winner throws the pallino.

- Toss is valid if the pallino passes center line and does not touch the back wall on opposite end.
- If the player fails to place the pallino in valid area, the opposing team will put the pallino in play.
- If both players fail, the pallino returns to the original team for an additional attempt. Alternating process continues until pallino is in valid position.
- The Team that originally tossed the pallino will play the first ball.

The Game!

- The first ball may be rolled by ANY member of the Team that originally threw the pallino—winners of coin toss or previous frame.
- Should the rolled ball hit the backboard without touching the pallino, it is a dead ball and removed from the court.
- The same Team must throw again and continue rolling until a valid point is established.

- Once the point is established, the opposing Team must point or shoot until they make a new (closer) point.
- Players may use side boards at any time.
- Balls can be measured at any time and, in case of doubt, an official referee or Tournament Official should be called. In the event a tie is determined, the last Team to roll a ball must roll again until the tie is broken.
- If after all balls are played there is still a tie, no points are awarded and play resumes with the Team last scoring tossing the pallino from the opposite end of the court.
- In the event a ball/balls are moved during a measurement by an official, the balls are returned to approximate positions and official will still make the call. If however, a member of a Team currently playing measures and moves a ball, the point is awarded to the opposing team. In any case, the decision of a referee or official is final.
- One Team Member can cross the centerline to measure balls. Other players need to remain at their respective end of the court.

Backboard:

- If a ball hits the backboard without first touching another ball or pallino, it is a dead ball and removed from the court.
- If a ball is shot, hits the backboard illegally and then strikes a stationary ball/s, the shot ball is removed from the court and the stationary ball/s are placed in their approximate original position/s.
- The pallino is always a valid target and remains in play even if it strikes the back wall after being struck by any valid ball during a frame. If however, the pallino is knocked out of the court or bounces back in front of the center line, the frame is considered void and the Team that started the frame will begin again at the opposite end of the court.
- In the event ball/s resting against a backboard are moved as a result of a valid shot, they remain in their new position. If however they move as a result of an invalid shot, they are returned to their approximate original positions.

Scoring:

- Only one team scores in a frame (unless there is a tie, in which case neither team scores)
- Games are usually played to 12 points
- Final games are usually played to 15 points (USBF recommended)
- Tournament Directors can decide any variation to game points but should do so prior to the start of the event.

Illegal movement of balls or the pallino:

- Players should never touch or move any ball or the pallino until the frame has ended. If a player moves a ball prior to the end of a frame (thinking play is over) and the balls cannot be accurately relocated to their positions, all remaining non-thrown balls of the non-offending team are counted as points. If the offense is committed by the playing team, all non-thrown balls of that team are voided and the frame is over.
- ALL players should be out of the court if possible. If not possible, they should be positioned in front of play area when a player at the opposite end is shooting.
- If a player is in the court standing BEHIND the point balls and pallino (In harm's way or "downstream") and is struck by a ball or pallino as a result of a raffa or volo shot, the opposing team receives the Rule of Advantage! The options are:
- Leave all balls and pallino in the new configuration, or
- Remove the ball or pallino that struck their opponent from the court. If the pallino is removed from the court, the frame is over and play begins from the opposite end, or
- They can place the ball or pallino that struck their opponent any where on the court.

If however, the player is standing in front of the point balls or pallino (Out of Harm's way or "upstream"), and is struck by a ball that moves backwards toward a player as the result of a raffa or volo shot, the ball remains in play because the player was in a valid position. In the event the pallino moves backward and touches a player the frame is over and play begins from the opposite end.

If a player is struck by a ball or pallino in a point attempt or lag, the Rule of Advantage applies no matter where the player was standing.

Shooting and Pointing:

- There are basically two (2) types of shooting.
- Volo: the act of lofting the ball in the air attempting to hit the target. Tournament Directors may, for safety concerns, determine that Volo shooting may not be allowed. If it is allowed the USBF uses the same foul line for both raffa and volo shooting.
- Raffa: the act of shooting at a target either by releasing the ball at ground level, slightly lofting the ball or rolling the ball in a force ful manner.
- Pointing is done with either foot or both feet before or on the pointing line. A throw is valid as long as any part of the foot/feet is on the line.
- When shooting (either style) the player is allowed to step on the line prior to releasing the ball. As long as even the heel is on the line, it is a valid shot.
- Once a player has released the ball, he/she is allowed to continue steps up to the center line. This is considered valid.

Late arrivals, substitutions, delays, etc:

- A team not present within 15 minutes of scheduled start of the game will forfeit the game.
- In a tournament where substitutes are allowed, a Team may substitute only once during a game and it must be announced to the opposing Team before the start of the next frame.
- A substituted player may not return to that game. If a player/s arrive late, the game will start with that Team playing shorthanded and minus the appropriate number of balls. Player may then enter game at "shorthanded" end after frame is completed. In the event a player must leave a game in progress, an alternate may enter at the end of a frame and the player that leaves cannot return for remainder of game. If no alternate is available, the game continues using the late arrival rule.
- Repeated "conferences" during a frame causing delays in the game

are discouraged. If delays continue, the offended Team Captain should notify an official.

- If an official issues a one-minute warning and delays continue, the "burned ball" rule should be placed in effect and one of the offending player's balls will be removed from the court.

Game Notes:

- Consecutive or alternating throws by teammates shall be at the option of the players.
- Any time a player is in action, opposing players should be off the court or far behind the player if courts don't have adequate space.
- If a player plays the wrong color ball, simply replace it with the correct color when it comes to rest. Play continues.
- If a player commits a foot foul while in the act of shooting volo or raffa, a warning is issued for the first offense. Should the same player foul again, the thrown ball is removed from play and all struck balls returned to their approximate original positions.

USBF NOTE: Unless there is a referee in the court, this would be a very difficult rule to enforce and should be addressed by the Tournament Director before tournament begins.

- If a player rolls/shoots out of turn or plays more balls than allowed, the opposing team has two (2) options. Leave all balls as they rest, or remove the illegally thrown ball from play and return all other ball/s to previous position/s.

Summary: The intent of the USBF Open Rules is to provide a guideline for playing a game of Bocce. These rules are used in all sanctioned USBF tournaments and are strongly recommended for any tournament at any level from social to competitive. For further information or questions regarding these rules, court construction, USBF events, etc., please contact the USBF @ www.bocce.com.

Chapter 11

International Play

Bocce is becoming increasingly more popular as a competitive, international sport, with enthusiasts lobbying for Olympic status. The good news is that the International Olympic Committee (I.O.C.) has officially recognized bocce, and this is a major step toward becoming an Olympic medal sport.

There are two sets of rules approved for international play – Punto Raffa Volo and Volo. In Punto Raffa Volo rules, the three different shots are allowed if executed according to the regulations, but under Volo rules only the volo and punto shots may be used. In other words, in the Volo game, if you decide to hit, you must loft, not roll your ball at the target. International Volo players generally use metal balls.

The international court is a large one, 27.5 meters long by 2.5 to 4 meters wide (approximately 90 x 13 feet) for Volo play. For Punto Raffa Volo competition, the court may be 24.5 to 27 meters long and 4.0 to 4.5 meters wide (approximately 80 to 88 feet long and 13 to 14.5 feet wide).

International rules are more complicated than open rules, but experienced players maintain that the regulations are not intimidating once you get acclimated. The international game is for purists, eliminating the element of luck. For example, you try to knock your opponents' point away with a volo, and your shot is off target, hitting another ball instead. This results, by chance, in your team winning the point. Purists reason, why should you gain an advantage with a poor shot? By international rules, if your ball didn't land within a specified distance of its target, it may be removed from play, and all balls disrupted by the volo attempt returned to their original positions.

As in the rules for other major sports, there is a *rule of advantage* option. Simply stated, if your opponent makes an illegal play which benefits your team, you have the option of accepting the result of the play.

In international games, referees mark the positions of live balls and, not unlike billiards, players call their shots. If a player attempts a knock-away shot and misses, displacing other balls in the process, those displaced balls may be returned to their original positions (which were previously marked on the court surface). Referees use a specialized measuring device/marking tool to spot the positions of balls and to trace arcs on the court surface. These arcs serve as boundaries for legal landing points for volo shots. As you might guess, these games take longer than those played with Open Rules. Tournament directors sometimes set arbitrary limits, such as declaring the game over at 15 points or 90 minutes, whichever comes first.

Proponents of the international game argue that a game to 12 points will not last any longer than an open rules game where many players delay the action by making frequent trips to mid-court to confer with teammates. International referees enforce a time limit between shots and forbid such delaying tactics.

Still, critics of the international style claim that it is too complicated and makes the game too long. The American people will prefer a quick and simple game, they maintain. And if a pro bocce tour ever comes to fruition, television coverage will demand a fast-paced, action-packed game. Others counter that, if bocce enters the Olympic arena, international rules will prevail. Americans should learn the game on the large court, and with the rules that will allow them to pursue the dream of one day representing the United States in international competition. Donna Allen of the USBF strongly recommends that any schools constructing courts build them to international specifications. "Build a backyard court to whatever dimensions fit your property and make you happy," she advises. "But build international-sized courts in the schools, and give our young people the opportunity to represent their country."

"You have to witness international rules compared to the open rules," says Dr. Angel Cordano, a retired pediatric researcher and bocce junkie who travels the world to compete. "It's the difference between chess and checkers." Cordano refers to international play as "the real game, where Mr. Luck is a third-rate citizen."

A Summary of the
PUNTO RAFFA VOLO REGULATIONS
of the Confederation Boccistica Internationale

Reprinted with permission of the
United States Bocce Federation

{This unofficial summary of the C.B.I. regulations was prepared by the United States Bocce Federation. It is intended only to be an abbreviated guide to the most frequently used rules. Any questions must be resolved by using the complete text of the official C.B.I. regulations}

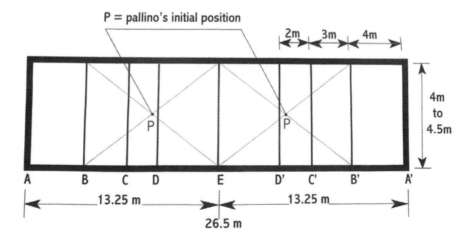

I. THE COURT. (See diagram)

Metric Conversion:

4 m = 13' - 1-1/2"

7 m = 22' – 11-1/2"

9 m = 29' – 6-1/4"

24.5 m = 80' – 4-3/8"

27 m = 88' – 6-3/4"

Lines A and A' = coincide with the end of the court and indicate the limit from which players can start their throw.

Lines B and B' = indicate the maximum limit allowed to the players to throw the pallino, the point shot, and the raffa shot. The opposite lines B' and B indicate the maximum distance the pallino can be thrown.

Lines C and C' = indicate the maximum distance allowed to the players for a volo shot.

Lines D and D' = indicate minimum distance a raffa shot must first touch the court, and the limit to which players can go when making a point shot, unless the player is out of balls.

Line E = (mid court) indicates the minimum distance that the pallino must be thrown, and the limit to which players can go when making a raffa or volo shot.

II. THE MATCH

Each match consists of three games. First you play three against three with each player having two balls. Next, you play a singles game, with each player having four balls. Finally you play a doubles game, and again each player has two balls. A substitution can be made at any time after a ball has been played. However, there are no substitutions in the singles game, and no player can participate in more than two of the three games in the match. Championship games normally go to 15 points, but preliminary rounds can go to 12 or 13 points at the discretion of the tournament committee. Only one team scores in a frame. One point is given for each ball that is closer to the pallino than the closest ball of the opposing team. The location of the pallino and balls of each team must be distinctively marked on the court by the referee.

III. STARTING THE MATCH

A. The Beginning

Each game of a match begins with the referee placing the pallino in the center of the court between the B & E lines. The winners of the coin toss may play the first ball, or choose the end from which to begin. If the choice is made to play the first ball, the opposing team can choose the end from which to begin. If the first ball played is invalid, the same team must play again until they have played a valid ball.

B. The Pallino

During the game the pallino is tossed by the winner of the previous round. If the toss is invalid, the opposing team tosses the pallino. If that toss is also invalid, the pallino is placed in the center of the court between the B & E lines by the referee. In any event, the first ball is played by the team that first tossed the pallino. You should always wait for the assent of the referee before tossing the pallino. The pallino toss is valid if it passes (not touches) the E line, stops before (does not pass) the B line, and does not touch or stop within 13 cm of the sideboard. If after a valid play, the pallino moves in front of or on the E line, or the pallino leaves the court, the play stops and is resumed from the original starting point.

IV. PUNTO, RAFFA, VOLO

A. Punto:

1. When pointing, a player's foot may be on but not over the B line. The roll is invalid if the player passes the D line after releasing the ball, unless the player is out of balls.

2. A ball that hits the sidewall without first hitting another object is invalid. The opposing team can apply the Rule of Advantage and leave the rolled ball in its final position or remove the ball from the court.

3. If there is a tie for point, the team last playing plays again until the tie is broken.

4. If the rolled ball hits another ball or pallino (object) and the struck object travels more than 70 cm, the opposing team can elect to return the struck object to its original

position and remove the rolled ball from the court, or leave all balls in their final position (Rule of Advantage). If several balls are struck and no single object travels more than 70 cm, everything is valid. If the rolled ball hits an object causing the object to hit the side or back wall, everything is valid unless the struck object traveled more than 70 cm (measured from original mark to the point of impact on the wall and then to the final position of the struck object.

5. If a struck object subsequently hits another object (chain sequence) and the distance from first point of impact to the final position of the last object is greater than 70 cm, the opposing team can apply the Rule of Advantage and leave all objects in their final position or return all objects to their original position and remove the rolled ball from the court.

6. A rolled ball that hits one or more objects which do not travel more than 70 cm, but the rolled ball travels more than 70 cm from the first point of impact, is an invalid throw. The opposing team can apply the Rule of Advantage and leave all objects in their final position or return the struck object or objects to their original positions. In either case, the rolled ball remains in play and is not removed from the court.

B. Raffa:

1. The raffa shot must be made from the B line, and the ball must first touch the court after the D line. If the mark made on the court by the impact of the thrown ball touches or "breaks" the D line, the shot is invalid.

2. Before taking a raffa shot, you must inform the referee that you intend to raffa and which object is your target.

3. If the raffa shot is invalid, the opposing team may apply the Rule of Advantage and leave all objects, including the thrown ball, in their final positions, or return all objects to their original positions and remove the thrown ball from the court.

4. The raffa shot must be released before the player's foot goes

over the B line (on the line is valid). The raffa shot is invalid if the player passes the E line after releasing the ball.

5. To be valid, the raffa shot must first hit the declared target or any object within 13 cm (about 5 inches) of the target (bersaglio).

6. You may raffa any ball including your own, provided that the declared ball is located past the D line. The pallino is always a valid raffa target no matter where it is on the court. The raffa shot can not be used on any ball located between the E and D lines unless the target ball is within 13 cm of the pallino (bersaglio).

C. Volo:

1. Before taking a volo shot, you must inform the referee that you intend to volo, which object is your target, and wait for the referee to mark a 40 cm arc in front of the declared target. The referee must also make a 40 cm arc in front of each ball located within 13 cm of the declared target.

2. The volo shot is valid if it strikes any object within 13 cm of the declared target, and the shot hits the court within 40 cm of the struck ball. If the mark made on the court by the impact of the thrown ball touches or "breaks" the arc, the shot is invalid.

3. If the volo shot is invalid, the opposing team can apply the Rule of Advantage and leave all objects including the thrown ball in their final positions, or return all objects to their original positions and remove the thrown ball from the court.

4. The volo shot must be released before the player's foot goes over the C line (on the line is valid). The volo shot is invalid if the player passes the E line after releasing the ball.

5. You may volo any ball including your own or the pallino.

A Punto Raffa Volo Rules Recap

As you can see, the international game is very different from the bocce most of us "hackers" know. Highly structured and a bit complicated until you get the hang of it, I think I have the hang of it, and here present my thoughts in the clearest English I can muster...{special thanks to Mike & Lois Conti, Joe Giolli, Ron Jacobs, Mike Grasser, Mike Lapcevich, John Ross, and Danny Passaglia who answered my never-ending questions}.

A true international match consists of a singles, a doubles, and a triples competition. You must win two of these three games to win the match. Winners of matches advance to play other winners until an eventual champion is determined. Sometimes tie-breakers (record against each other, most points scored, fewest points allowed) are needed to crown a victor.

The international court has a lot of lines. One is four meters from the end. This line is for pointing and raffa hitting. Raffa is the fast rolling style of hitting as opposed to the aerial volo shot.

For pointing you can have your foot on, but not completely over, the line. Some players walk forward after releasing the ball to ensure accurate momentum in the proper direction. Raffa players use a walk or run-up delivery. They also follow through by continuing forward after releasing the ball. In both pointing and raffa hitting, the ball must be out of the player's hand before s/he crosses the line.

A second line is another three meters forward. This is the volo line. Players use a longer run-up approach when they volo, hence the additional distance.

Two meters farther ahead is a third line which is the minimum distance a raffa shot must travel before it first strikes the ground. In other words, your raffa attempt must be lofted over this third line, then roll the rest of the way to its target.

Finally, there is a mid-court line beyond which the first toss of pallino must come to rest to begin each frame.

Let's call the end-board point A, and these previously described lines B, C, D, and E respectively. Down at the other end of the court you have another end-line A or A' if you like, as well as lines B, C, and D.

International rule makers don't want the pallino too close to the sideboards or too near the ends. Thus, the initial toss of pallino each frame may not come to rest less than 13 cm from either side board or beyond the B line at the court's opposite end.

The game is called Punto Raffa Volo because you can employ all three shots. But there are restrictions. The international rules committee decided that hitting an opponent's ball that is near mid-court is relatively easy for accomplished players, and declared the space between line E and the other end's line D to be the volo zone. If you want to hit a ball that rests in that area, you must do so via volo.

You may raffa anywhere beyond that volo zone (the greater the distance the tougher the shot) and you may volo anywhere on the court (volo generally is more difficult than raffa). Also, you may raffa the pallino no matter where it lies on the court.

The referee marks the position of every ball on the court's surface. If an errant shot is made, the balls can be returned to their previous positions.

Players who want to hit a ball away must call their shots. On synthetic surfaces the referee uses chalk to mark the positions of all balls and the pallino. You must call which ball you will hit and whether you will do so via raffa or volo. If you declare that you will raffa one ball and hit another by mistake, the Rule of Advantage applies. That is, your opponent can decide to let the play stand, or put the displaced balls back where they were and remove the raffa attempt from play. Exception - if the ball you hit was within 13 cm of the declared target, all is forgiven. This qualified as a *bersaglio*, and is therefore a legal hit.

The referee uses a brush to erase previous chalk marks.

If you call a volo shot, the referee traces an arc 40 cm in front of the ball you intend to hit. Your ball must land within that arc for it to be a valid hit. If not, the Rule of Advantage applies and the other team may either leave the play as is, or "burn" the ball and replace all the displaced balls to their previously marked positions.

When I first viewed international play, the trajectory for most volo attempts was lower than I anticipated. Players tell me that the lower shot doesn't bounce as high, which means you can be a tad short and still hit your target. Also, the higher the toss the greater the distance the ball travels. A greater distance makes for a greater degree of difficulty.

Some Rules and Points of Emphasis

If you hit the backboard without first hitting another ball, your ball is dead and removed from the court. When the pallino is close to the end line where it is difficult to lag without hitting the back wall, a player often rolls his ball short (just past the volo zone) so that he or his teammate can raffa it to the end with the next shot. For good hitters, this is easier than out-lagging a point near the end where you have to worry about striking the back wall and "burning" your ball.

You may not hit the sideboard (Rule of Advantage applies).

All balls must be in the rack unless it is your turn, and you are about to roll. The referee and opponents, by checking the rack, can easily see how many balls are still to be played.

After you have played all your bocce balls, you are to move to the mid court area (this lets everyone know that you have no rolls left this frame).

Players stay on the court while teammates or opponents play their shots. Although they might inadvertently interfere with play, players stand to the side and closer to the end from where the shot is originating. Displaced balls tend to move away from them, not toward them. In addition, all balls are marked and can easily be returned to their proper positions.

The referee's "stick" can be used to measure, mark the positions of balls, and scribe the arcs for volo attempts.
Jeff O'Heir photo.

You must ask the referee's permission to come down court to view the positions of previously played balls. Fail to do so and you forfeit one ball.

The referee uses a 70 cm tool for measuring and marking. If the referee holds this tool straight up (perpendicular to the ground) he's indicating that you took the point with your last roll. Holding it in a horizontal plane means the other team is still in.

The tool has a sliding section that can be used to measure. Players can ask the referee how far away a ball is and s/he can illustrate the distance by holding the tool up to the players' view.

Some Stickier Points

Displacing another ball even when you are pointing can create a Rule of Advantage situation. If your ball taps another ball causing it to move a distance greater than the length of the tool (70 cm) the rule applies (with fast-playing surfaces, it doesn't take much of a hit to move a ball 70 cm).

Moreover, if your ball moved the pallino just a short distance and caromed off to hit another ball, and that ball moved more than 70 cm, the other team has the option of putting the pallino back to its original position, but the displaced ball stays put.

Bersaglio – when a ball is within 13 cm of the pallino or when two balls are within 13 cm of each other, a bersaglio exists. This means you can call your shot and hit either of the two balls to make a legal hit. Also, you can raffa when there is bersaglio no matter where the balls are. Because of this, sometimes a pointer doesn't want to get too close to the object ball. For example, if the ball was 14 cm away and in the volo zone the opponent would have to volo. But if it were 13 cm or closer they could raffa.

A Summary of the VOLO REGULATIONS
of the Fédération International de Boules

Reprinted with permission of the
United States Bocce Federation

{This unofficial summary of the F.I.B. regulations was prepared by the United States Bocce Federation. It is intended only to be an abbreviated guide to the most frequently used rules. Any questions must be resolved by using the complete text of the official F.I.B. regulations}

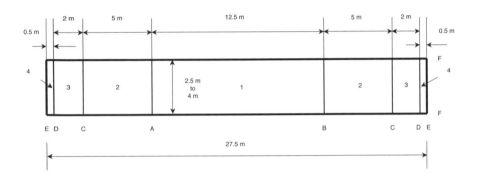

I. THE COURT

CROSS LINES:	AREAS OF THE COURT:
A – foot line	1 – 12.5 meter rectangle or center area
B – first line	2 – 5 meter rectangle
C – second or maximum line	3 – 2 meter rectangle
D – third or back line	4 – back area
E – fourth or end line	
F – side line	

METRIC CONVERSION:

0.5 m = 1' – 7-11/16"	2.5 m = 8' – 2-3/8"	12.5 m = 41'
7.5 m = 24' – 7-3/16"	27.5 m = 90' – 2-3/8"	

II. STARTING THE GAME.

The right to toss the jack in the first end (frame) is decided by a coin flip. Subsequently, the team winning an end tosses the jack. Any member of a team may toss the jack without being obliged to play the first ball.

The delivery is valid when the jack comes to rest in the 5m rectangle opposite the end from which it was tossed (between the B and C lines). If a team fails to validly toss the jack after two attempts, the opposing team places the jack where it wishes within the square, as long as it is at least 50 cm from all boundary lines of the square.

In any event, the team which tosses the jack must play the first ball. The opposing team plays until they take the point or play all their balls. If the first ball goes out of play or is annulled, the opponent must play. If their ball also goes out of play, the first team plays again, and so on. If no balls are left on the court after a valid roll or throw, the opposing team must play. If this last ball played goes out of play or is annulled, the other team must play again, and so on. When each team has a ball equidistant from the jack, the team that played last plays again. If the tie is not broken, the other team plays and so forth until the tie is broken. If a player plays someone else's ball by mistake, simply replace it with the correct ball.

An object is out of play if its central circumference passes beyond the outer limit of the line (side line F, or third line D) or touches the side wall. The jack is also out of play if its central circumference does not reach past the first or B line.

III. ROLLING THE BALL

Every ball must be played within a maximum time of 45 seconds which starts from the time when:

a) the jack is correctly placed in the court;
b) it has been decided which team shall play;
c) the referee has made his decision;
d) the required replacements of displaced objects have been made.

In case of infringement the referee will at once annul the ball and it must not be played. If it is played it has no effect.

A rolled delivery is regular when the ball:

a) does not go out of play;
b) reaches to at least 2 meters from the first line;
c) does not move any object more than 50 cm from its original position;

These three conditions must all be satisfied at the same time.

IV. THE THROW

The player who wishes to throw (or shoot) must clearly designate the object which is the intended target. There can only be one target, and it may not be a ball of the player's own team. A mark will be drawn by the opponents 50 centimeters in front of the designated object. This mark must be curved and from 15 to 20 cm in length. Every mark which is not challenged before the throw is valid for checking the point of landing. When the designated object is surrounded by other objects, the curved mark must extend in the necessary direction. Additional throw marks must be made in front of each object situated less than 50 cm from the designated object, providing that such marks are within a circle concentric to the external perimeter of the object and placed 50 cm away from the object.

A throw is regular when all three of the following conditions are met:
   a) the point of landing is not more than 50 cm from the desig-
      nated object;
   b) the point of landing is not more than 50 cm from the object
      first struck;
   c) the object first struck is not more than 50 cm from the desig-
      nated object (measured from the maximum diameter of the
      objects in question);

The outer edge of the throw mark must not be modified or erased by the impression left on the court by the thrown ball at its point of landing.

A throw is also regular when a ball strikes directly, i.e. without having first touched the court, an object positioned at not more than 50 cm from the designated object. However, in the case of a regular throw with a non-designated jack, the jack is compulsorily restored to its original position.

V. THROW AT THE JACK

If, during an end, the two teams still have one or more balls to play, the jack may be designated once by each team. (This does not apply when balls still to be played belong to only one team.) If the declared jack is struck by a regular throw and there are still un-played balls belonging to both teams, the end is nullified and will be played again in the same direction. In this case the jack is thrown by the team that had originally thrown it. A non-designated jack hit by a regular or irregular delivery is always replaced to its original position.

If only one team has balls remaining and a declared jack is struck after a regular throw, the throwing team receives one point for each ball that has not yet been played. There is no restriction on the number of throws which may be made on the jack in this situation, except that the last remaining ball may not be thrown at the jack.

VI. ADVANTAGE RULE

All irregular deliveries are left to the discretion of the opposing team. It may:

a) accept the whole new situation thus created, and can either accept or annul the irregular ball;

b) demand the general replacement of all objects to their original positions with the compulsory annulment of the irregular ball.

VII. POSITION OF PLAYERS

In all cases, when not rolling or throwing the ball, all players must stand to the side of the square where the jack is positioned, one team on each side of the court, beyond the first line. At the moment of the throw, the players must stand still and not stare at or do anything to distract the thrower. If space permits all players will keep off the court, as near as possible and along the side line.

A Volo Rules Recap

I first witnessed Volo play at the US Bocce Championships held at the Highwood Bocce Courts, Highwood, Illinois. The Highwood courts have a fast-playing synthetic surface that might have been damaged by volo shooting (volo entails tossing metal bocce balls into the air in an attempt to displace an opponent's ball or the pallino). If you want to hit a ball, you must first call your shot, then strike it with a volo attempt – no raffa, or fast rolling hitting is allowed.

The tournament directors put down a temporary carpet to protect the synthetic surface. This inevitably produced a few surface bubbles as well as some complaints from participants, but the event was extremely well-run and the carpet necessary for the venue to safely host this event.

Each end of the court is marked with three white lines. From the back wall these measured .5 meter, 2.5 meters, and 7.5 meters. Any ball that passes the ½ meter mark is "dead" no matter how it gets there. To begin a frame, the pallino must come to rest between the 2.5 and the 7.5 meter lines. Also, the 7.5 meter mark is the foul line for both pointing and hitting.

It is a little easier to "zone in" for pointing in this game since the object ball is always within a couple meters of the same place. In Open Rules, for example, you could place the pallino anywhere from mid-court to the back wall – a big variation if you are playing on a long court.

When pointing, your foot must be completely behind foul line (as opposed to the other international game - Punto Raffa Volo - where your foot may be on the line).

The side walls are dead (court surface is canted at both sides to minimize chances of balls hitting sides). European volo courts often have no sideboards.

If the pallino touches the boards the frame is over.

One of the top American volo players, Benji Tosi, struts his stuff at the World Championships in Torino, Italy.

Every hit must be a Volo, whereas in (Punto Raffa Volo) a fast-rolling hit (raffa) can be employed.

When you call a shot, the referee scribes a 50 cm arc in front of the target ball. Your ball must land within this arc to be a valid hit, otherwise the Rule of Advantage applies. A volo that lands on the line delimiting the traced arc is invalid. Restrictions are the same as in Punto Raffa Volo play except you cannot call your own ball. Also, unless you designate the pallino as the target, a displaced pallino is always returned to its previous position whether or not the volo shot was valid.

No matter how the balls are scattered by the called shot, we can tell by the arcs if the ball fulfilled the necessary requirements. The referee can check the mark left by the ball when it struck the court surface. If the ball struck a ball on the fly, the referee can view the marked position of the ball that was struck.

Rule of Advantage, as in Punto Raffa Volo play, means that the offended team can take the result of the play or "burn" the illegally tossed ball and replace all displaced balls to their previous positions.

If a rolled ball results in the displacement of any object a distance equal to or greater than 50 cm, the opposing team may "burn" the ball and return the moved balls to their previous positions.

Note: the positions of all balls are marked.

After rolling or shooting you must go to the other end so as not to interfere with the next player's roll.

Some Final Volo Points

The metal volo balls (brass or other alloy) are a tad smaller than the traditional 107 mm plastic composition balls and some contain a special rubber material in the core that absorbs bounce. So, you can hit just in front of the target and, instead of bouncing over, your shot is likely to strike its intended target.

When pointing, you don't have to worry so much about displacing balls 50 cm, as their mass and composition is such that they don't roll too far after being struck, even on fast surfaces.

Sometimes it is difficult to distinguish one team's bocce balls from another's (colors are similar), but distinctive lines etched on the balls' surface make for easy identification on closer inspection.

Variation in the size and weight of balls is allowed within certain parameters.

Games are long – matches may go to a set number of points (generally 13 or 15) or to a time limit (1 ¼ hours to 1 ½ hours) or to whichever comes first.

Special Events
(Precision Shooting - Rapid Progressive
Shooting – Combination Event)

Some international competitions feature "shoot-outs" reminiscent of the NBA three-point shoot-out. Officials place balls in different positions and at different distances from the shooter (using a specialized mat which has eleven different positions at which a target ball or pallino is placed). The balls are side-by-side, one in front of another, even behind the pallino. One to five points are awarded for successful hits based on the degree of difficulty for the particular shot. For this Precision Shooting, players generally get two attempts at each target, proceeding in a pre-determined sequence, and keep a cumulative score. Contestants can rack up a maximum of 37 points.

The Rapid Progressive Volo Shooting is an event where target balls are placed on pre-positioned locations on mats located at each end of the court. The contestant runs to the 7.5 meter line and lofts his shot at the target, and then runs to the other end, picks up a ball from a stand, and repeats the process back in the opposite direction.

There are six target spots on each mat located .8 meter apart. After each hit, the target ball is placed in the next position (.8 meter farther away). After the last target is struck, the targets are moved progressively forward and so on. The exciting event lasts 5 minutes.

Contestants in this event are physically fit and train like 1500 meter track athletes. John Ross of the USBF informs us that the world record is 52 hits in 54 attempts, adding… "Imagine a 1500 meter runner throwing a 2-1/2 lb. ball every 30 meters along the way and hitting a 4 inch target 40 to 60 feet away with 98 to 100% accuracy!"

To recap, for this event a mat is used, upon which are placed target balls. As a player makes a good hit, the target is progressively moved farther back from one to six designated spots on the mat. When you hit the first target, a "spotter" places the target ball in the second position on the mat. (There are six positions on each mat, and a mat at each end of the court. You have five minutes to run back and forth, hitting as many targets as you can within the time limit. It is ironic that, to the uninformed, bocce conjures up images of old, out-of-shape wine drinking, cigar smokers, while this demanding event rivals any cardiovascular endeavor one can imagine.)

The Combination Event

The combination event consists of eight frames. One contestant lags the pallino. Once the object ball comes to rest, a 70 cm radius circle is drawn around it.

One contestant then lags into the circle using the pallino as a target. If the ball enters and stays in the circle, one point is earned by the lagger. The other contestant then shoots, attempting to knock the ball out of the circle. One point is awarded for each hit. Each player has four balls. At the completion of the first frame, they resume from the opposite end except that the contestants reverse roles.

There are always four shots in every frame. A "par" score would be 32, but two points can be earned if the lag comes within .5 cm of the pallino or touches the pallino.

Also, if the shooter's ball stays within the circle after a successful hit, 2 points are awarded. Even if you don't aspire to compete at the international level, this is an excellent way to practice your volo and pointing skills.

A Final Note: Not many North Americans are playing this volo game. If you set your mind to it and practiced hard, you could become skilled at this event, and compete at a high level. The numbers are in your favor. Contact the United States Bocce Federation at www.bocce. com for info on how to get started.

The combination event is played one against one, with each player having four balls. The winner of the coin toss throws out the pallino and selects whether to lag or shoot in the first frame. The player not lagging will be the shooter in the first frame. The players will alternate roles in the second, third, and fourth frames, i.e. the lagger becomes the shooter, and the shooter becomes the lagger. In the fifth frame, players do not alternate roles. The player lagging in the fourth frame will lag the balls in the fifth frame. The players then alternate roles in the sixth, seventh, and eighth frames.

The pallino will be thrown by the same player for two consecutive frames, even if the player is the shooter in a frame. The first player throwing the pallino will throw in frames 1, 2, 5, and 6. The other player will throw the pallino in frames 3, 4, 7, and 8.

Points are scored as follows:

After the pallino comes to rest with the box, a 70 cm radius circle is drawn by the opponent using the center of the pallino as the center of the circle. If the pallino comes to rest less than 70 cm from the side, the center of the circle is moved laterally toward the middle of the court so that a full circle can be drawn. In this case, the pallino remains in place where it came to rest, offset from the center of the circle. The lagger rolls a ball and must land completely within the circle. If the ball is invalid, the player lags again. All invalid balls are removed from play. The lagger receives one point for each ball completely within the circle, and two points for a ball landing within one half of a centimeter from the pallino ("biberon"). When the first valid ball is within the circle the pallino is removed, a 50 cm arc is drawn, and the shooter attempts to knock the ball out of the circle. The shooter will continue to shoot until a valid hit is made. After a valid hit, the lagger will roll another ball. The shooter receives one point for each ball knocked completely out of the circle, and two points if the shooter's ball remains completely within the circle ("carreau"). If the lagger failed on all four attempts to make a point, one of the lagger's balls is placed in the center of the circle to provide a target for the shooter. Also, if the lagger is out of balls, the shooter may attempt a maximum of two shots on the pallino. If the pallino is knocked out of the circle, the shooter receives two points for each hit.

{This unofficial summary of the F.I.B. regulations was prepared by the United States Bocce Federation. It is intended only to be an abbreviated guide to the combination event. The complete text of the official F.I.B. ITR must be used for additional information or resolution of questions.}

CHAPTER 12

THE BEST OF *THE JOY OF BOCCE WEEKLY*

Background

In 2002, I began launching a weekly electronic newsletter. Initially emailed to about 1000 bocce aficionados, circulation quickly increased by nearly ten-fold. Connecting bocce players from around North America (with a smattering of international subscribers as well), the publication continues to flourish.

Early on, we got noticed by email publishing industry professionals. Janet Roberts, who writes a popular column for electronic newsletter publishers (Ezine-Tips.com), made reference to "Mario Pagnoni, who publishes an infectiously enthusiastic email newsletter called the Joy of Bocce Weekly..."

Writing in Best Ezines Issue #115 - June 5, 2002, Ms. Roberts said...

"If you don't play bocce (an Italian bowling game), you'll want to run out and find the nearest court after reading this enthusiastic ezine. Mario Pagnoni claims not to be a bocce pro, but you wouldn't know it from his devotion to the sport. Each issue of the HTML ezine (with graphics and colors) features his personal comment on some aspect of the game and its players, highlights of coming tournaments and detailed evaluations of new bocce products. The ezine also fosters a feeling of community in the bocce world by including reader comments and a photo section each week. Whether you learned to play in your Uncle Joe's backyard court or you're looking for a new sport to master, Joy of Bocce will point you in the right direction."

Initially, I was unsure about maintaining a weekly deadline. One reader, an ezine publisher himself, cautioned me about how ambitious an undertaking a weekly would become. He was right of course. But it has been a labor of love.

My primary goal was, and still is, to promote the game we love, and to be a voice for unifying the sport. It irritates me that horseshoes (a good game, but one that can't hold a candle to ours) is so well standardized while American bocce still struggles to get to that next level.

Joy of Bocce Weekly subscribers took to the ezine right away…

"I think your weekly e-mag is a wonderful idea and will go a long way to further popularize this excellent sport that combines social as well as athletic skills. I look forward to the next edition." Sal Fauci - Endicott, NY

"I wish you well on this new endeavor. Anything anyone can do to help promote the sport helps fulfill the goals of the United States Bocce Federation."
Donna Allen - USBF

"Thanks for keeping the game alive. You will always have support from here."
Rich Mazzulla - Elmwood Park, IL

"I welcome your *Joy of Bocce Weekly.* I'm the Texas Special Olympics Director of Bocce Competition." Ed Crozier

"Hey Mario--- Great newsletter! Keep 'em coming." Jeff Jernstedt - Portland, Oregon

"Your Ezine was a welcome surprise for the New Year, and I think a good idea." - Stan Stanton - Las Vegas, NV

Referring to the standard "opt out" language for ezines, Peter Ferris of Coweta, Oklahoma wrote…

"I thought 'bocce' and 'unsubscribe' were mutually exclusive! You shouldn't use them in the same sentence!"

Ray DiCecca of Wilmington, MA offered...

"I very much enjoy your weekly newsletter, and look forward to reading my e-mail every Monday morning, knowing that the latest "Joy of Bocce" will be waiting for me. It's great to have one location collecting as much information as you do on such an enjoyable subject."

DiCecca inquired about back issues which prompted me to implement an archive system at www.joyofbocce.com (Back Issues).

You can "opt in" to receive *The Joy of Bocce Weekly* by visiting www. joyofbocce.com and adding your email address to any of a number of subscription links sprinkled throughout the web site. Your subscription will bring you bocce stories, comments and suggestions on bocce play from readers around the globe, tournament listings, and easy access to our most popular "Photos of the Week" feature.

Bocce Quotes of the Week

A regular column called Bocce Quote of the Week became an instant hit with readers. Following are a couple favorites...

It's Easy!

Our Monday morning outdoor bocce season is often hosted by yours truly. My wife, pictured on the home page of www.joyofbocce.com (displaying outstanding bocce form, I might add), runs a family daycare home. The kids always know when it's bocce day. They come outside for recess and chant "Bocce! Bocce! Bocce!" lead by four-year-old Ryan Hamilton.

The adult players arrive at 9:00 am. We have coffee and pastry, then play games separated by short breaks for more libations and more food. We eat. We play. We eat some more. Ryan, already an avid sports fan (New England Patriots, Boston Red Sox), became so enamored of the game that he asked for a bocce set for Christmas. Santa delivered.

Recently he taught his parents and sister how to play. "It's easy," he said. "First you eat. Then you roll some balls. Then you eat again!"

****

Intermission

We are constantly looking for "new blood" for our Monday morning bocce sessions. Most of us are retirees, and we try to recruit younger players. Recently, we've added some twenty- and thirty-year-olds to the fold. We play several games, enjoying coffee and pastry between matches. After a spirited match, octogenarian Del Bracci, a former National Super Senior Downhill Ski champ said "Nice game... time for an intermission."

One of the "young pups", an athletic, energetic type and first-time bocce player, chimed in with, "Intermission? For crying out loud - the entire game's an intermission!"

Okay, bocce might not be a cardiovascular workout. But the pastime's regimen of gentle exercise, friendly competition, and camaraderie are just what the doctor ordered. And never underestimate its value as a lifetime sport - one you'll not have to abandon as you age.

****

Close, But No Cigar!

During one hotly contested match, one team made a great roll, the ball coming to rest touching the pallino. It was Tom's turn next, and he never hits, preferring to lag no matter how close the other guy's point. He rolled deftly, making a terrific shot – his ball also "kissing" the pallino.

We examined the situation, trying to wedge a credit card or dollar bill between the balls. No doubt about it. It was a "dead heat."

We told Tom to roll again, because, although he had tied the other team's point, he hadn't beaten it. Confused, Tom ambled down the court to take a look for himself. He peered from one angle, and then took another vantage point. He squinted, scratched his head, and finally spoke. "Sure, they're both touching" he announced... "but mine is definitely closer!"

****

Chess/Bocce

When I introduced bocce to my friend Walter, he took to it right away. A competitive, athletic type, Walt likes softball, racquetball, and karate. He particularly enjoys the strategic aspects of bocce, like leaving a ball in front to block, tapping the pallino to another, more advantageous position, and thinking ahead a move or two. This cerebral aspect of our sport is missed by most beginners. They enjoy playing. They begin to get better at the sport. But, once they see the broader picture - that the game involves tactics and maneuvers that require advance planning, they are hooked.

Sure, you still need good touch and finesse, some occasional brute force, and even a little luck, but this is a pensive person's pastime. "This game is a lot like chess" says Walter. "The problem is, I know where I want to put the pieces, but I can't always get them there."

****

The Joy of Bocce and the Arts

Long-time promoters of bocce, Rico Daniele and I had similar questions when asked to run a bocce event in the Arts District of Chattanooga, Tennessee. "They play bocce in Tennessee?" asked Rico, while I countered with "You mean to tell me they have an Arts District in Chattanooga?" Surprisingly (and fortunately), the answer to both questions is Yes! And Dr. Charles (Tony) Portera is the man largely responsible. A transplanted Mississippian, Portera is one of the South's leading cancer surgeons. The man has a staunch passion for medicine and the arts, an unwavering vision about what he wants for his city, and a firm grasp on his roots. Together with his wife Mary and their family, he has conceived and developed the Bluff View Arts District, a classic conclave of cafes, gardens, museums and galleries.

Nestled in one of the city's finest historic areas, Bluff View features bed and breakfast in elegantly restored homes (circa 1900), gourmet dining in any of several restaurants (fresh made pastas, pastries, and chocolates), and culture in the River Gallery and the outdoor Sculpture Garden featuring local as well as nationally known artists' work.

Gazing over all that comprises the Arts District, including the gorgeous, well-manicured bocce court overlooking the Tennessee River, renowned oncologist Portera declared "I deal with death every day - I did this for joy."

Readers' Feedback

The ezine serves as a sounding board for players who make comments, ask questions, and offer suggestions.

Journeyman player Dr. Angel Cordano's vote of confidence read... "Congratulations for the enjoyable *Joy of Bocce* that I eagerly read every week. You are doing a great service to our sport by exposing what's going on all over the US."

Sometimes there are questions I can answer myself...

Steve Kahn from Banning, CA ...

> "We old codgers are having a mild argument. One side says that all team members shoot from one end of the court, and then all walk to the other end and shoot again. This is obviously a must for singles.
>
> The other side says that for two-person teams one member of each team is at each end. For four-person teams two members of each team are at each end. In either case, nobody walks. Which is right?"

My answer...

> Whichever way you decide to play is right. There is no hard and fast rule for this. I prefer a little walking to get some exercise. Also, there is more camaraderie when all of the players are at one end...and, when walking

end to end, you play every frame instead of every other one.

The only time we stay at one end is when we play 4 vs. 4. Two teammates are stationed at each end, rolling two balls each. An alternative would be to keep all 8 players at one end, roll one ball each, and walk end to end.

Sometimes there are questions a reader can answer...

Someone asked about a game with 3 players in an "every man for himself" or "cut-throat" mode. What would determine the order of play in such a match?

Self proclaimed "Bocce Bum" Ben Musolf of California shed a little light on the question...

> "We play cut-throat all the time. The rotation of play is as follows. First you determine who goes 1st, 2nd, and 3rd. Then it is the same as regular bocce. Whoever is farthest away from the pallino goes. We play up to 30 points where the closest ball gets 3 pts, second gets 2 points and the third gets 1 point. Therefore, you can score up to 6 points in the round if you have the three closest. We only use three balls each though."

I usually add my two cents worth - {my comments in brackets}

> {Thanks Ben. This clears up the rotation of play with three players. Whichever of the three is farthest away must roll the next ball. The scoring is unorthodox in several ways. Score three, two, and one points for the three closest balls instead of just one point each...and more than one player can score in a round – in fact all three could score...interesting. Now we'll need a scoreboard to track three players' totals. A final thought...

we need a better term than "cut-throat" for this style of play.}

Another question answered by a reader...

"Do you have to roll your last balls when you have the game winning point and the other team is out of balls? Can you drop them at your feet?"

I've seen players toss their remaining balls a couple feet in front of the foul line to signify that they are done playing and the match is won. If they were to play a ball they might "sell the point" as they say. That is, they might knock an opponent's ball closer or hit the pallino and give away the point (I don't know where the selling part comes in).

Mike Conti of the United States Bocce Federation supplied the answer...

"When Yogi Berra made the comment 'It's not over until it's over' he also meant when it's over it is over. When you win you want to celebrate and thank your opponents for a good game, not drop balls in front of their face - that's like rubbing it in."

We get comments that inform...

I found that many of our readers dabble in other outdoor games as well as bocce. Quite a few subscribers are avid pétanque players.

Jan and Louis Toulon of Toulon Imports and the Pétanque Mariniere Club of San Rafael, California enjoy pétanque or boules, as it is sometimes called. Similar to bocce played with small metal balls, I learned the game while in Holland and found it quite enjoyable. The only complaint I had was that it was often difficult to tell which ball belonged to which team because the variation in color is not striking. You really had to pay attention to which ball was tossed by which player.

Tom Grow from The TX Hill Country says "We rotate Croquet,

Horseshoes, Bocce & Badminton - Bocce always dominates (goes better with wine)."

We learned about people in carpeted office buildings playing bocce on their breaks and lunch hours. The down time is too short for them to get to the gym and back, and the brief diversion (mental and even a tad physical) is just what the doctor ordered. One advocate of the practice declared it perfect for "high powered business types who want to compete, but don't want to work up a sweat."

We get compliments...

Jim Mancini of Visalia, CA writes...

> "I'm about halfway through your book – I skip around – and it is terrific. Everything I wanted to know and then some. And you write clearly and concisely."

Sometimes we get compliments and a feeling that we made a difference...

Dick Gomez from Northern California...

> "Thanks for the great newsletter and web site. I also have to thank you for your book, *The Joy of Bocce*. My wife read it at least six years ago, and it changed her game completely. She was a one night a week, play for fun, wine, and food type player, but after she read your book, she became more interested in the game, and has become a most excellent lagger. She's a tournament champion, and still retains her passion for the game (as do I)."

There are always questions about court construction.

The award for Best Advice to a Prospective Court Builder goes to Mike Hoban of Raleigh, NC. Says Hoban, "Build it and they will come... with beverages."

We get opinions...

"The US has innumerable players scattered all over, playing almost independently on their local turf and it is time to get together in order to become a world power. I would like to see that we play with similar size and weight bocce balls of 107 mm and 920 grams, since those are the official measurements at world level competition."

We get complaints...

"Why can't we get TV exposure for our game so that we can reach a wider audience?"

{Television exposure is just what this game needs. There is a ground-swell of activity with this wonderful sport that needs to be harnessed and pointed in the right direction.}

Sometimes we get the word out on bocce happenings...

The Dating Story (which airs on The Learning Channel) filmed a "bocce date" in New York City. We alerted readers to the episode's airing date and time, and later offered this recap.

The episode was filmed at Washington Square Park and several boules and bocce players who are "regulars" at the park were happy to coach the couple (and get in front of the camera).

Caroline, from Hoboken, New Jersey, and Carmine, of Staten Island, had a passing familiarity with bocce.

Carmine, a 28 year-old letter carrier and Caroline, a 31 year-old real estate agent studying nursing in the evenings, seemed to hit it off pretty well on this their first date.

Before the date, Carmine's friends teased him with the following banter...

"She's gonna whip your butt in bocce."
"Maybe her school's got a bocce team."
"Yea, maybe she's a pro."
"Maybe she's putting herself through school with bocce."
"I think I read about her in Sports Illustrated."

Caroline just ended a relationship and is "holding out for the right person." She aptly described their dating scenario as "an interactive game of bocce."

One of Caroline's friends wisely counseled her that "Bocce will show if you are compatible or not."

Although they seemed a little confused about how to play and how to keep score, it was obvious that Caroline and Carmine enjoyed the game and each other's company.

When they parted company, Caroline wrote her phone number on a Post-it note and handed it to her date. True to his word, Carmine called her. The TV episode closed with Caroline's statement that "I can't wait for our second date."

We sometimes review other interesting bocce web sites...

While cruising around the Internet recently I came across (http://bocce.baltimore.md.us).

The webmaster (Thom LaCosta) has created an entertaining and well organized bocce site containing details on Baltimore's bocce action as well as general information on the sport.

I particularly like the web site's section on the History of Bocce. Like other historical accounts (and lore) it quotes Sir Francis Drake who is purported to have said of the rapidly advancing Spanish Armada..."First we finish the game, then we deal with the Armada." But this is the first time I have come across the following light-hearted and very amusing account credited to Michael Kilian of the Chicago Tribune...

"Some historians claim bocce dates back 7,000 years. The Egyptians played it when they weren't struggling with pyramid stones, and the Romans picked it up from them (I don't think Cleopatra did, however, as it's not a game you can play in bed).

The barbarians within the Roman Empire took a liking to it – the Gauls producing a French version called "boule." The English, who never quite got the hang of things, turned it into the tacky pastime you see on television's Championship Bowling.

Unlike Championship Bowling, bocce is not a game of roll, slam, crash, rack and have another brewski. It's a true sport involving skill, finesse, strategy and cunning."

Finally — and best of all — we reprint photos...

Subscribers from all over the world send photos of their bocce venues, court construction or tournament action. We post the photos on the web site each week and link to them via the ezine. These are the "Photos of the Week." By far the most popular part of the publications, these pictures provide insight into the world of bocce — different types of courts, kinds of constructions, and styles of play. We love viewing other people's bocce courts, and we enjoy seeing others reveling in the joy of bocce.

sometimes it's just you and the pallino

Photo by Elizabeth Jade Wong Fontana

Sometimes bocce lends itself to great works of art. This one by bocce aficionado Frank Ansley (www.FrankAnsley.com).

Sometimes we use bocce to help raise funds for great causes.

Sometimes my bocce posse and I run parties,
corporate outings, and team building events.

Sometimes we start them young.

Sometimes they learn
to volo early on.

Eventually, all experience *The Joy of Bocce!*

About the Author

Mario Pagnoni published the highly successful *Joy of Bocce Weekly*, an ezine connecting bocce aficionados everywhere. The author of several sports, computer and education books, Pagnoni has written for *The Boston Globe* and *Referee Magazine* among others A retired public school teacher and coach, he runs bocce tournaments, bocce fund-raising events, corporate outings, and parties with bocce as the focal point. Find out more at www.joyofbocce.com